The Philosophy of Law

The Philosophy of Law

An Introduction

THOMAS MORAWETZ

MACMILLAN PUBLISHING CO., INC.

New York

COLLIER MACMILLAN PUBLISHERS

London

Macmillan Publishing Co., Inc.
866 Third Avenue, New York, New York 10022

Collier Macmillan Canada, Ltd.

Library of Congress Cataloging in Publication Data

Morawetz, Thomas (date)
  The philosophy of law.

  Includes index.
  1. Law—Philosophy. 2. Law and ethics. I. Title.
K231.M67   340.1   79-15767
ISBN 0-02-383340-8

Printing: 1 2 3 4 5 6 7 8   Year: 0 1 2 3 4 5 6

To my mother

Acknowledgments

This book grew out of my courses in the philosophy of law at Yale University. My first debt is to my teaching assistants and students, both at Yale and at the University of Connecticut School of Law. Joel Feinberg urged me to convert my course lectures into a book, and I am deeply grateful for his continuing support, advice, and stimulation. I am also indebted to Ronald Dworkin and Robert Fogelin, who shaped my interest in the philosophy of law and ethics, first as teachers and then as professional colleagues.

My friends Charles Larmore and Stephen Holmes read large sections of the manuscript and made suggestions of great value. I appreciated an opportunity to revise the manuscript after Richard Wasserstrom's perceptive reading of it. Finally, I am grateful to my research assistant, Marcia Gleeson, and to Mildred Mobilia and the secretarial staff of the University of Connecticut School of Law for their efficient and indispensable help.

Contents

Introduction

What is most familiar is often what is most puzzling.
Can we adequately describe the nature of physical objects, the character of thought and feeling, or the
difference between sleep and wakefulness? One way
of describing the job of philosophers is to say that they
identify the mystery of what is familiar and then try to
understand and dispel the mystery. Thus, philosophers
of law recognize that it is one thing to be familiar with
laws and legal systems, but it is another to be able to
analyze the concept of law. It is one thing for a judge
or lawyer to use legal reasoning, but it is something else
to stand back and describe legal reasoning. It is one
thing to hold persons legally responsible for their actions but something else to be able to say what responsibility is.

Philosophical inquiry has immediate effects on life
and conduct. Judges who study legal reasoning are likely

1

to carry out their job with heightened awareness of the resources appropriate to decision making. They will be more likely to engage other judges in debate about the purposes of legal systems and about the limits of their own job in realizing those purposes. The citizen who has looked into the nature of responsibility may not be more responsible, but he or she will come to appreciate the dilemmas and compromises of criminal law and the complexity of human conduct.

Many of the problems of legal philosophy are problems of normative political philosophy. This means that they involve inquiry into what the relationship between persons and governments ought to be. Some writers argue that governments exist to benefit their citizens and that any governmental action is justifiable to the extent that it contributes to general well-being. Others argue for a more limited role for government. They say that individuals are to be seen as having rights and that the actions of governments are limited by these rights. No action is justifiable if it interferes with the enjoyment of rights. In this view, governments exist to see that rights are protected and to promote well-being only when doing so does not involve infringement of rights. Both of these theories, the theory of rights and the theory of maximal benefit, give primacy to individuals and argue that governments exist to serve individuals. Other theories give priority to the state as an end in itself.

Such political theories have direct implications for the decisions of judges and legislators. Legislative debate is about the desirability of particular laws, but it is also about what kind of society is best and about the proper relationship of government to its citizens. Similarly, the merits of a judicial decision involve the merits of the particular view of society and of the role of law that the decision exemplifies. The choices of a legislator and of a judge are ethical choices and have ethical consequences. To debate about legal reasoning one has to address ethical reasoning. We shall see that many disagreements among legal philosophers are disagreements about the nature of ethics or about the place of ethical considerations in legal decisions. Because such philosophers often fail to unpack and examine all of the assumptions they are making about ethics, I shall introduce my discussion of judicial and legislative decision in Chapters 2 and 3 by analyzing several theories of ethics.

One important theme in the philosophy of law is the attempt to distinguish normative from descriptive questions about law. So far, I have referred to normative questions, questions about how one assesses laws and legal systems in terms of their purposes and how one evaluates the performance of judges and legislators. One can lay aside these preoccupations and consider the formal features of laws and legal systems. Describing law as an institution by picking out its formal characteristics has been an important and challenging task throughout the history of jurisprudence. Many writers have stressed the importance of keeping separate the analysis of the institution from any consideration of the uses to which the institution has been or may be put. They emphasize the logical priority of knowing what something is before considering how it is used or abused.

Political and legal philosophy were dormant in the United States and England for a long period after World War II. The revival of philosophy of law around 1960 was stimulated by H. L. A. Hart's attempt to offer a new formal account of the concept of law. Before discussing Hart's theory, I shall try to explain what philosophers do when they analyze concepts. I shall also trace the history of debates about the concept of law. We shall see that these debates often appear to be between those who claim to give a formal account of law and those who argue that any such formal analysis must fail because moral principles are part of law and a formal analysis will leave them out. This debate is about both the nature of law and the use of the term *law*. It uses the tools of both metaphysics (the study of the nature of things) and philosophy of language.

The philosophy of law not only overlaps ethics and political philosophy, and metaphysics and the philosophy of language. It also borrows issues and arguments from philosophical psychology and the philosophy of action. What assumptions about human nature are we making when we hold persons responsible for their actions? In what circumstances are persons not responsible for what they do? Answers to such questions are an essential part of an explanation of law and they require investigation of the nature of will and action. Accordingly, just as I have used part of Chapter 2 to make clear ethical reasoning, I have tried in Chapter 4 to analyze the notions of will and responsibility. These discussions go beyond philosophy of law strictly so-called, but they are indispensable for understanding the context of legal institutions, a context defined by the understanding of human nature, human society, and personal and social obligation that philosophers in various domains have tried to achieve.

Much is now being written in the philosophy of law. Any attempt to summarize the most important themes of contemporary legal philosophy runs two risks. It may reflect the particular interests of its author and the writers he has found most cogent. And it may become dated as new circumstances create new issues in philosophy of law and cause perennial issues to be addressed in new ways. But these risks are unavoidable.

1
Philosophy and the Concept of Law

•

What Is the Philosophy of Law?

In 1961, Professor H. L. A. Hart of Oxford University published *The Concept of Law*. The book had a remarkable impact. It resurrected philosophy of law in England and America, where (along with ethics and political philosophy) it had been dormant for about twenty years.[1] Hart began his book by pointing to the remarkable fact that modern writers have over and over again asked the question "What is law?" as if the project of defining law had to be started anew. Let's see why this has been so.

When philosophers ask "What is law?" they assume

---

[1] See Peter Hacker and Joseph Raz, editors, *Law, Society and Morality: Essays in Honor of H. L. A. Hart* (Oxford, 1976), Introduction.

5

that their readers already know how to identify laws. They are not asking for a definition that will help persons to recognize law, as a definition might help persons to pick out armadilloes. They are looking instead for a description of a special kind, one that in ordinary circumstances is neither offered nor sought by those who are involved in the day-by-day activities of the institution of law.

A philosopher of the kind I have in mind seeks presuppositions. The characteristic philosophical insight is that an institution (like law or science) has presuppositions that go unquestioned by practitioners and are implicit in their activity. Philosophers elicit and examine these presuppositions.

A comparison with the philosophy of science will help to make clear what it is that philosophers of law do. The practicing scientist and the informed layperson may take for granted that science is progressive and convergent, that we advance in a more or less linear fashion over the history of science in the direction of knowing more about physical reality. The philosopher of science makes this belief explicit and discusses whether it is indeed logically presupposed by science. Is science progressive? Do we know more about the world than scientists did in ancient Greece, or do we just know more about what interests us and less about what doesn't? What tools are available to answer this question? The philosopher of science uncovers and examines other presuppositions. For example, scientists make discoveries, present theories, and so forth. The philosopher, in contrast, asks about the *nature* of discovery and what it is like to construct, offer, and test a theory.

The same can be seen in the philosophy of law. The practicing judge assumes his decisions must be just; at the very least he pays lipservice to this assumption by being prepared to argue that these decisions are just.

The client determining his tax liability or seeking to comply with the statute of wills assumes that the law is what the statute says it is, whether it is just or not. The philosopher's job, in turn, is to ask whether both are right in their assumptions and to explain what relation between law and justice is presupposed in the institution of law. Another example: the judge, the penologist, and the layperson all assume that we can and must distinguish offenders who are responsible for their actions from those who are not responsible by reason of insanity or coercion, or because they acted inadvertently, and so forth. The job of the philosopher is to ask how we make this distinction, whether it is drawn consistently across different kinds of cases, and whether it is susceptible of justification.

It is evident that philosophers intend their descriptions to be abstract and general. Unlike historians, philosophers are concerned with particular and concrete events (legal events, scientific events) because of what they show about law and science in general. They aspire to give an account that is descriptive of every instance, e.g., an account of the criteria of responsibility that can explain every proper application of the notion. An excellent example of this kind of investigation is Joseph Raz's recent book, *The Concept of a Legal System,*[2] in which Raz gives general criteria for the existence of a legal system ("What is presupposed in saying that a legal system exists?"), for the identity of a legal system ("What distinguishes one system from another?", "By what criteria do we say that laws belong to one system or another, to the same system or different systems?"), and for the features of a law ("Does every law impose a duty?", "Is every law addressed to a citizen, or to an official?"). The investigation is intended to be perfectly general.

[2] Oxford, 1970.

The example of Raz's book points up an important
distinction. When I say that philosophers look for presuppositions, I am not saying that they look for things
that persons consciously think and believe. It would be
possible that no one, lawyer or layperson, has ever
thought about Raz's questions; perhaps those who have,
even experienced law practitioners, have not been able
to answer them. These practitioners do not have presuppositions in the sense of answers-in-reserve. But such
questions must have *some* answers. Their answerability
is *logically* presupposed in the ongoing activities of law.
Either it is the case that all laws impose duties, or it is
not.[3] An answer is logically presupposed whether it is
consciously considered by a practitioner or not. This
means that although philosophers seek presuppositions,
they do not report the beliefs of practitioners; they do
not poll scientists and tell us what they think science is,
or lawyers and judges to tell us what they think law is.
It is a common mistake to say that they do.[4]

This mistaken conception confuses some of the
philosopher's raw materials with his results. Whatever
practitioners say about responsibility, for example,
philosophers must ask whether the line between responsibility and nonresponsibility is drawn consistently
from case to case. Is it arbitrary or justifiable? Does it
make sense to say that the law may be just or unjust,
or that the law has nothing to do with justice?

[3]We shall see that some positivists in the nineteenth century claimed
that all laws imposed duties; later refinements of positivism involved the
view that there are many different kinds of laws, only some of which
impose duties.

In a sense, this either/or statement is misleading. The materials of law
can always be *translated* into a scheme that is such that all laws do impose
duties. As we shall see, such a scheme may be very awkward and may
do little to illuminate the character of law. But the theorist has a choice
and the materials do not determine an either/or answer.

[4]This mistake is well displayed in Chapter 7 of Herbert Marcuse's book,
One-Dimensional Man (Boston, 1964). The modest self-descriptions of
some linguistic philosophers have fostered this kind of misunderstanding.

The mistake I am discussing comes from thinking of a philosopher as a kind of empirical investigator, specifically as an investigator of what persons say and think about what they do. These data, when available, are among the raw materials of the philosopher as documents are the raw materials of the historian. The philosopher's final accounting is a critical interpretation of the data, because he submits the raw data to tests of consistency, coherence, and justifiability.

Consider a hypothetical case in which the Supreme Court is asked to interpret the due process clause of the fourteenth amendment of the Constitution. The issue, let us say, is whether a state is required to provide legal counsel for indigent defendants who cannot afford a lawyer's fee.[5] Assume that in federal courts counsel must be provided because this is required by the sixth amendment. Consider four judges writing opinions on this issue. Judge A says that the due process clause merely requires states to set forth some announced procedure for disposing of criminal cases and to follow that procedure uniformly and visibly from case to case. The job of judges, in his view, is to apply the plain meaning of whatever rules happen to be put forward in the constitution and by legislators. Judge B says that judges are required to interpret and apply the intentions of those who drafted the fourteenth amendment. He concludes that they intended to incorporate the right to counsel within the fourteenth amendment, and that state practice must therefore conform. Judge C, on the other hand, concludes that the due process clause requires judges to exercise and unpack their *own* sense of fairness and that it was the intention of its authors that they do this. It follows, she says, that counsel is required because fairness dictates this. Judge

[5] Compare the actual Supreme Court case of *Gideon* v. *Wainwright,* 372 U.S. 335 (1963).

D takes a different position. He concludes that it is the nature of law that it be just and fair, and that it is irrelevant whether legislators did or did not intend the law to be applied justly. He resolves the case by examining the notions of justice and fairness, by looking at the rights of persons, and decides that all persons have the right to be represented by legal counsel.

These judges have different views not only on the question posed by the case but also on the nature of law and on the role of judges. Judge A thinks that law is whatever legislators say it is, whereas Judge D believes that law necessarily embraces justice. Judge A thinks that the job of judging is limited to applying the letter of the law; Judge B disagrees and thinks that judges must uncover and carry forward legislative intent, whatever that intent may happen to be. Judges C and D, unlike A and B, are convinced that judges must take account of moral considerations, but C, unlike D, would limit the judge's introduction of these considerations to those issues for which the legislators invite them to do so.

The job of philosopher of law is to look at each of these views analytically and critically. Is the view that law is whatever legislators say it is plausible? What are its assumptions and implications? How would it be justified? Why would one be tempted to challenge it and suggest that law is what legislators say it is *only* if what they say is just and fair? Can *this* view, and the assumptions about human nature and politics that lie behind it, be justified? In the same way, the various distinct opinions about judging can be examined. To do so is important for two reasons. It not only helps us to understand legal systems and the purposes that they can and should have, but it also confronts those who have power and authority over the lives of persons, judges and legislators, with the challenge of examining and justifying their everyday activity.

Law and Conceptual Analysis

Recent philosophical essays and books have such titles as "The Concept of a Person," *The Concept of Mind,* and *The Concept of Law.*[6] The authors ask "What is a person, mind, or law?" and say that they are doing conceptual analysis. Let's look at what conceptual analysis is and at why some recent philosophers have argued that it is a fruitful and creative way of doing philosophy. Let's also look at different kinds of concepts to see what kind of concept "law" is.

I shall first choose a simple concept, "knife," to explain how conceptual analysis is carried out. It goes from the commonplace to the surprising, from what we've known all along to discoveries about our particular concepts and about the nature of concepts and of thinking in general. To have a concept is in part to be able to use certain words correctly, to pick out instances of that to which the word refers, and to make certain appropriate kinds of judgments and discriminations. If I have the concept of a knife (or a car), I ordinarily can talk about knives (and cars) and can pick out knives from spoons and bottle-openers (and cars from trucks and tanks). What I look for will vary with circumstances: a rubber stage prop will not count as a knife in some situations but will do fine in others. Still, there is a family of characteristics that most knives will have in most circumstances, and I will look for these features in picking out knives.

Among the characteristics I will look for is cutting ability. It will probably be on the basis of this criterion that I will reject the rubber prop when I do so. But is a knife that hardly cuts at all a very bad knife or not a knife? Note that there is no obvious answer: in some

[6] A. J. Ayer, *The Concept of a Person and Other Essays* (London, 1968); Gilbert Ryle, *The Concept of Mind* (London, 1949); H. L. A. Hart, *The Concept of Law* (Oxford, 1961).

contexts I will say one thing and in others another, and the answer will depend on how obviously important cutting ability is in the situation. This is important because it shows that we don't have one set of characteristics for knives and another for good knives, the latter to be used in distinguishing good knives from bad ones. Anyone who has the concept of a knife can also pick out good knives for standard purposes. This is generally true of artifacts. Knives are artifacts that serve purposes, and it should not be surprising that the concept of a knife includes some reference to the purposes it serves. Thus, "cutting well" is not just a feature of good knives but a criterion of knives-in-general, part of the concept of a knife. What we have is something like a family of criteria whereby "good knife" defines a higher threshold than "knife," because we can be satisfied in a given context that something is a knife but a bad knife for contextually related reasons: it hasn't satisfied the higher (more demanding) threshold.

Having seen this, we can make (1) a general point about philosophy and (2) a specific point about the analysis of the concept of law. (1) The general point is that in describing a concept, a philosopher may unpack norms that are implicit in the concept, criteria for judging and evaluating objects. Consider the difference between "A good knife has a blue plastic handle" and "A good knife won't break when used to cut." The first expresses a personal preference and is a disguised piece of autobiography. The second is not autobiographical at all and will be conceded by anyone who knows how to use the concept of a knife. The second is the kind of description the philosopher is after.

My purpose here is to dispel a common misconception. This is the view that there is a strict separation between conceptual facts and values. According to this view, one can either describe by way of a concept (can say what knives are) or express values as preferences.

I am suggesting, to the contrary, that a description of a concept may *include* values. A philosopher may *refer* to norms without making normative judgments in the sense of setting forth *new* rules for using the concept or expressing personal preferences. It seems plausible that the view that description and conceptual analysis cannot properly involve a reference to norms involves the following confusion between artifacts and natural objects. Simple artifacts generally have a standard function in normal contexts; natural objects do not.[7] One may be able to identify and characterize cats and rocks without any notion of what is a good cat or a good rock. One needs to ask "Good for what purpose— for throwing, for use as a paperweight, for studying limestone crystals?" (Natural objects have inherent purposes only if nature itself is conceived teleologically.) Of course, I am not saying that an artifact has a *single* purpose. A knife can be used in many ways in different contexts. I *am* saying that an object that has come into existence through human agency is such that we can always ask "Why was it made?" and "What can be done with it?" And our understanding of what it is, i.e., what sort of thing it is, depends on our being able to answer some question of this kind.

Why does this matter? We shall see that the most basic division and the most interesting controversy among those who analyze the concept of law is about whether the concept can be explained without reference to inherent moral purposes and to such values as justice and the recognition of rights. To take what is called a "positivistic" approach to the concept of law is to insist that an account need not and should not include reference to any substantive moral content for law. A

---

[7]It is disputable whether artistic productions have a standard function. I shall include enjoyment, enlightenment, and so on, among possible artifact functions and shall assume for present purposes that artistic works have these functions.

positivist says that the most illuminating and satisfactory account identifies law by formal features, such as that law is a system of rules, promulgated by those with power and authority, backed by sanctions, and regulating public behavior. A naturalist would challenge this account as inadequate. Typically, a naturalist insists that the notion of law involves not only posited rules, whatever their content may be, but a concept of shared public purposes and a set of critical moral standards. We shall return to this debate and examine it from several perspectives.

(2) Obviously my primitive dichotomy between artifacts and natural objects does not account for all or most concepts of things. It is useful for the limited purpose of raising the question of what kind of artifact a legal system is. The question is much more complicated than the parallel question about knives. On the one hand, legal systems seem to differ from knives in being more complex artifacts; in this view, there are *inherent* purposes for both knives and legal systems. We can imagine a commission of scholars of law asked to create a legal system for a new state. They must do so with certain explicable purposes in mind. On the other hand, legal systems rarely come into being in this way; typically they are created, used, and abused for varied and conflicting particular purposes. It is not obvious that legal systems in general have any specifiable universal function in ordinary contexts in the way that knives do. Perhaps legal systems have a second-order purpose, namely that of creating order and structure in human society so that individuals may come together to pursue varied and conflicting purposes. Perhaps even this kind of purpose is not *inherent* in the concept of law. Perhaps legal systems have frustrated diversity in human activity as often as they have fostered it.

Obviously, we must not lose sight of the historical dimension of discussions of the concept of law. If we choose to say that law has an inherent general purpose, for example something as general as the welfare of the governed, we must recognize that the appeal and plausibility of this claim is shaped by our history. Our ideas of government, of the relation of the individual and the state, and of the capacities of persons are products of our cultural history. What we say about the concept of law and what social experiences we use to test our concept are not likely to be the same as what would have occurred to an ancient Greek or a seventeenth-century Frenchman. But this does not mean that our concepts "law" and "legal systems" refer only to our own laws and legal system. Rather they are the terms we use in identifying and talking about laws and legal systems in general, historical and contemporary.

Philosophers who offer accounts of the concept of law differ from each other in two ways. As we have seen, they disagree first with regard to whether an account requires some reference to the purposes and goals of law. I shall try to explain in detail why positivists have insisted on doing without such reference, indeed without any reference to the necessary content of a legal system, and how this insistence may be explained by noticing a distinction between artifacts like knives and artifacts like legal systems.[8] Second, even philosophers who *agree* that an account of the concept of law must be partly purposive (teleological) will usually disagree about the identity of these purposes.

It is important to remember that claims about the purposes of law are not simply claims about observable data. It will not do, therefore, to refute the claim that the purpose of law is to achieve and insure justice by taking a survey of legal decisions and showing that many results are unjust. This is irrelevant just as it would be irrelevant to refute "Knives are made for cutting" by

[8] See pages 38–51 of this chapter.

showing some very blunt knives. (Note that I am not
arguing that the claim that there is a conceptual link
between law and justice is true, but only asking what
kind of claim it is. It is a conceptual claim and not a
straightforward empirical one. The link, if there is
one, will have to be one that allows for the fact of unjust interventions.)

One clarification. Different thinkers will carve their
domains within the philosophy of law differently. They
will attend to different questions. I am not claiming
that *every* analyst of the concept of law will have to
consider the purposes of law and in particular the
relation of law and justice. Again, a comparison with
knives is helpful. A cataloguer of knives may define
them in terms of shape, structure, materials, method
of manufacture, and so on, with no concern at all for
their purposes. Similarly, some philosophers of law are
concerned with analyzing the concept of law with attention to the definition of a law, the criteria for the
existence and identity of a legal system, and the structure of a legal system, but with no attention to the
content of a legal system or the question of univeral
goals and purposes. (Raz's book is a good example of
this kind of inquiry.[9]) Moreover, such an analysis may
be justified in excluding reference to content and
purpose because these matters are controversial. This is
a warning not to confuse (a) philosophers who discuss
the concept of law but decline to talk about the purposes of law with (b) philosophers who deny that law
has inherent purposes or any universal content. A debate about whether law is an artifact and, if so, whether
it is an artifact with inherent purposes is a debate about
position (b).

---

[9] Raz discusses the content of law at several points where questions of
content are inseparable from questions of structure. He states as the aim
of his book to discuss questions of structure and form rather than questions of content.

Perspectives on the Concept of Law

Hart's *Concept of Law* is a defense of a positivistic theory of law. It is also a critique of earlier positivistic theories and an attempt to define the aims and limits of a theory of law. Before looking in some detail at how he does this, we need a few preliminary distinctions. The first distinction is between an internal and an external point of view toward law. Hart argues that an adequate theory of law must describe an internal point of view. In explaining what this may mean, I shall borrow Hart's terminology and some of his examples.[10]

Consider first the point of view of an investigator who describes social behavior by recording the frequency with which certain overt patterns of movement occur. A being from another planet might take this approach to us, as we would take it toward, say, a colony of ants. Accordingly, such an investigator of human behavior could record the frequency of behavior of going-into-movie-theaters-on-Friday-nights and the frequency of behavior of stopping-at-red-lights and decide that both were equally frequent occurrences. There would be no reference to the fact that behavior of either kind would or could involve intentions or that the behaving creatures were self-aware. By analogy, an anthropologist may describe primitive tools simply as found objects. This is the most extreme sense in which an observer of social occurrences and artifacts may be an external observer, external to the *intentional* character of the behavior. If we use the term *action* for intentional behavior, we can say that ants merely behave, whereas

---

[10] Hart seems to me ambiguous in his definition of the internal point of view. At different points in his discussion, having an internal point of view seems to mean (1) being able to deploy the notion "rule" and "obligation," (2) being subject to a legal system, and (3) having the characteristic attitude (acceptance) of one who is the subject of a legal system. Hart does little to clarify this ambiguity.

persons act. The external observer in this sense of "external" doesn't distinguish action from mere behavior.

An observer may use the notions of action and intention and still be unable to distinguish frequent movie-attendance from equally frequent stopping-at-red-lights in the important sense in which only the second is the kind of action that is governed by law. Hart points out that an observer of law must be able to distinguish acting out social *habits* from following social *rules*. "If a social rule is to exist, some at least must look upon the behavior in question as a general standard to be followed by the group as a whole. A social rule has an 'internal aspect' in addition to the external aspect which it shares with a social habit and which consists in regular uniform behavior."[11]

We can conclude that to be able to identify legal systems and to begin to characterize the concept of law, an observer must have an internal point of view in the sense of having not only the concept of action and the concept of intention but also the concept of a (social) rule. Thus, we can begin an account of law by saying that a legal system is a collection of social rules of a particular kind. (I have not yet specified the kind of rule so as to distinguish legal rules from rules of games, rules of etiquette, and so on.) None of the legal systems that a theorist observes need be the observer's own, the system to which he himself is subject. But he is "internal" to law in two senses. As a person who is aware of his own intentional actions and sees others as actors, he is "internal" to an awareness that human action is intentional. The observer also has some experience of being subject to laws as rules and is able to generalize that experience. This means that even when the systems are not his own, he will be able to make reference to the *characteristic* attitude and situation of persons subject

[11] Hart, op. cit., p. 55.

to law and of persons who regard themselves as subject to law.

I have spent time on this because Hart claims as one special merit of his own analysis of the concept of law that it takes account of the internal point of view.[12] Before looking at this feature of his analysis, let us consider the general purposes and outlines of his account. In giving an account of the concept of law, Hart sets out to solve the following problem. If we assume that a legal system is a set of social rules, what distinguishes it from other kinds, like rules of etiquette, or rules set by a nonlegal coercive force, like a gunman? Hart thinks that certain formal characteristics of legal systems distinguish them from other systems of rules and he draws attention to those features. He says that in a legal system there are two kinds of rules, rules at two different levels. He calls them primary rules and secondary rules. Primary rules are what one thinks about immediately as examples of laws. They tell ordinary citizens to do or refrain from doing particular things. Secondary rules, on the other hand, "provide that human beings may by doing or saying certain things introduce new rules of the primary type, extinguish or modify old ones, or in various ways determine their incidence or control their operation."[13] Rules about forming legislatures and conducting courts are all secondary rules. One secondary rule has special importance. Because the set of primary rules changes over time, one must be able to tell what the valid primary rules of a legal system are at any point in time. The special secondary rule that represents this criterion is the rule of recognition. A primary rule, in Hart's terms, is *valid* if it meets the criterion described by the rule of recognition.

[12] Ibid., pp. 55–57.
[13] Ibid., p. 79.

What purposes motivate Hart's analysis? What specific problems is it said to resolve? (1) The first problem is best explained by looking at the history of legal positivism. Hart is building his theory on the shoulders of other positivists. All of them stressed the importance of the fact that law is a matter of coercive rules, orders backed by threats and obedience commanded by power. Hart is a sophisticated positivist; he is aware that law is not simply a system of coercive rules but a special kind of coercive system. Specifically he takes note of the pitfalls in the theory propounded by John Austin in the nineteenth century.[14] Austin offered a positivistic analysis of law in which laws were compared to the commands of a gunman; Austin's "gunman" was a sovereign whose power was such that his commands were habitually obeyed, and who owed obedience to no one. The point of Austin's analysis was that unlike rules of etiquette or games or morality, law was a system of generalized coercive rules emanating from a central and absolute power-holder.

What was wrong with Austin's theory? Hart points out at least three difficulties.[15] All the difficulties stem from the claim that law emanates from a personalized holder of absolute power. One objection to any simple Austinian theory is that laws generally have transpersonal continuity; that is, they generally survive the death of any particular person who is the sovereign. By Austin's account it would be hard to see how this could be so. Another objection is that laws often apply universally across society and to the makers of rules as well as to ordinary citizens. The sovereign theory provides no obvious account of this possibility; the sovereign can hardly be commanding himself. Let's call

---

[14] John Austin, *The Province of Jurisprudence Determined* (London, 1954) (originally published, 1832).

[15] Hart, op. cit., Chapter 2.

this the problem of self-limitation. It is best illustrated in legal systems like that of the United States which have a constitution that limits legislative powers. In Austin's model, it would be incoherent for the lawgiver to have limited power, for a command to be unconstitutional and therefore not law. The third problem grows out of the first two. It is that Austin defines legal authority and legitimacy in terms of power, the power to issue and enforce commands. But power and authority are distinct concepts. We recognize unusual situations in which an invader or usurper of the state has power but not authority, and in which the unseated legislators still have authority to issue laws but no power.

Hans Kelsen, working in the 1930s and 1940s, tried to apply some of the methods of European social science to the analysis of law. He produced a positivistic theory that meets some of the problems that Austin's theory failed to meet. Kelsen's theory is an advance over Austin's insofar as it does not assume that a legal system is a collection of laws (and that laws are simple commands) but treats the overall structure and source of a legal system as needing a more complex analysis.[16] In Kelsen's theory coercive laws (norms backed by sanctions) come not simply from a sovereign, from whoever has a monopoly of power and exacts obedience, but from a basic norm (Grundnorm) that defines the legitimate or authorized source of laws. Just as for Hart a rule is a valid rule if it is recognized by the rule of recognition, for Kelsen a norm is a law if it emanates from the Grundnorm.

The notion of a Grundnorm is not altogether clear. According to some interpretations, Kelsen's point is

----

[16] Hans Kelsen, *General Theory of Law and State* (Cambridge, 1945); *The Pure Theory of Law* (Berkeley, 1967). Raz makes this distinction between Austin and Kelsen in *The Concept of a Legal System*, p. 4.

psychological. A Grundnorm exists insofar as a person regards some source as authorized to make rules and in this formal sense deserving to be obeyed.[17] Not every holder of power is regarded in this way; the gunman or usurper of political power is not. In this view, the existence of a Grundnorm is a matter of attitude on the part of those who are commanded. Austin ignores the problem of psychology and therefore puts forward an inadequate theory. A different interpretation of Kelsen's view would say that it is not simply a psychological account. The existence of a Grundnorm is usually *reflected* in the attitudes of persons, but it is not the same thing as a set of attitudes and is not reducible to a set of attitudes. In this second view, persons could be mistaken in attitude: a Grundnorm could exist and not be recognized as such. This view has its attractions. It allows us to say of a conquered people that has been heavily propagandized that they may believe the conqueror is authorized to give law but they are wrong. The psychological account would not allow us to say this. But the cost of the second view is high. It does not tell us what legitimacy and authority are or how one knows whether a Grundnorm exists. I emphasize this point because it is important to an understanding of Hart. His theory is in part an attempt to overcome this difficulty.

Even Kelsen would have to admit that the line separating a holder of power from an authorized holder of power is indistinct. A new usurper of power is legitimated if he holds power over time, if his subjects come to think of him as authorized, if he is recognized by other governments to be legitimate, if he sets up and maintains stable institutions, and so on. All these difficulties notwithstanding, Kelsen's theory overcomes

[17]See Joel Feinberg and Hyman Gross, *The Philosophy of Law* (Encino, 1975), p. 6.

many of the unsolved problems of Austin's theory. Commands are laws when they proceed from legitimated power. The notion of the Grundnorm is one whereby legitimacy (lawmaking power) may be lodged not in a person but in an institution (Parliament and the Queen), in a document that creates an institution (the Constitution of the United States), or elsewhere. Thus, the Grundnorm allows Kelsen to account for continuity beyond a particular sovereign and for self-limitation: the paradox of one setting rules for oneself disappears if we think instead of a constitution that sets laws (and limits upon permissible legislation) for all persons.

Although Hart's rule of recognition plays a role similar to that of Kelsen's Grundnorm, there are several differences between their theories. We have seen that Kelsen defines the existence and limits of a legal system in terms of an insufficiently defined point of origin, the Grundnorm. Hart, on the other hand, explains the structure of a legal system in terms of ongoing internal relations among primary and secondary rules. It is intrinsic to Hart's analysis that the system of laws is dynamic, that it can and will change over time.[18] Kelsen saw correctly that a legal system consists of norms of behavior and an authority norm (Grundnorm) defining the legitimate source of ordinary norms. But he did not place the authority norm within a family of secondary rules that prescribe how authority is to be exercised and how the system is to be changed.[19]

We can now see why and how Hart tries to do the

---

[18] Although there is this similarity between Kelsen and Hart, Raz points to an important distinction. Kelsen, like Austin, defines the existence of a law simply in terms of its origin (in the Grundnorm) whereas Hart defines its existence in terms of its on-going internal relations to other rules, the secondary rules of the legal system. Raz, *Concept,* p. 120.

[19] Although Kelsen claims to offer dynamic as well as static principles of individuation with regard to legal materials, this analysis is reducible to his so-called "statics" of law. See Raz, *Concept,* pp. 112–114.

positivist's job of formally defining law better than
Austin or Kelsen. He agrees with Austin that law involves coercive rules of duty and obligation, but he
insists that they are only part of a legal system. He
borrows and generalizes Kelsen's idea of a secondary
norm, a rule whereby rules of duty and obligation are
recognized as duly constituted (valid), and he expands
the idea into an analysis of a whole family of rules
about rules, rules about the making and changing of
rules. In this way, Hart claims to account for continuity,
universal reference, the possibility of constitutional
self-limitation, and change in the content of law. I shall
discuss criticisms of Hart's analysis on pages 28–38 of
this chapter.

(2) The second kind of contribution that Hart makes
to the positivist tradition is that, more than Austin and
Kelsen, he takes account of the internal aspect of law.
This means, for Hart, that law is not only (a) a system
of primary and secondary rules but also (b) a system of
social rules toward which those who are subject to the
rules have a special kind of attitude: they use them in
mutual criticism, regard them as authoritative, and so
on.[20] Here, of course, Hart is suggesting the same point
as Kelsen, that there is a characteristic psychological
attitude of those who are part of a legal system, whether
as citizens or obeyers. We need to address the point with
care. What *is* the psychological aspect of legal rules?
Can Hart persuade us that the attitude *is* an essential
feature of law?

To begin with, it is easy to misunderstand Hart's
point. In referring to the internal aspect of law, he is
saying more than that individuals use a rule of recogni-

---

[20] It could be argued that Kelsen refers indirectly to the internal aspect
when he refers to the role of Grundnorm in relation to other norms. But,
unlike Hart, he does not talk about the Grundnorm being *regarded* or
used in any particular way; he simply says that it exists and is the source
of legitimacy, and so on.

tion to identify the rules that apply to them. The internal aspect is more than the attitude of an observer identifying the laws of a system by reference to a rule of recognition *plus* the added awareness, "This applies to me." By the "internal aspect" of law, Hart seems to mean that a significant number of citizens regard the laws as duly authorized and do not regard the governing power as usurped. In psychological terms, the point is that citizens internalize the law as a standard for themselves and for judging others.

We can pursue this line of argument by looking at the way in which Hart distinguishes among three characteristics of laws and legal systems: the *validity* of laws, the *efficacy* of laws and legal systems, and the *acceptance* of laws and legal systems. *Validity* refers to the standing of primary rules vis-à-vis secondary rules; a primary rule is valid if its pedigree is in accord with the system's procedures for making and changing laws. A rule may be valid and lack efficacy. That is, it may be a valid rule that is not regularly obeyed. One may speak of the efficacy of legal systems as well as of the efficacy of particular laws. In this sense, *efficacy* refers to the standing of a system of primary and secondary rules vis-à-vis (a) the general fact that most rules are obeyed and (b) a general attitude of internalization. According to such positivist theories as Austin's, a legal system is efficacious if there is general obedience. But because there may be general obedience even to a gunman, Hart characterizes an efficacious system by discussing the internal aspect, saying that it involves *acceptance* of the valid rules.[21] At the same time, Hart recognizes that no legal system is likely to win universal acceptance. Some citizens will have the attitude toward the law that they would have toward a gunman, and no individual will be likely to internalize every rule set

[21] Hart, op. cit., Chapter 6.

down. But a system is only marginally a legal system if most persons most of the time obey only out of fear.

A different misunderstanding of Hart would be to confuse what he calls the internal aspect or acceptance of laws with a judgment of *moral* approval of such laws. One can have an internal attitude in the required sense of accepting authoritative rules and still be critical of their advisability and effects. One may disagree with the moral position of particular legislation without rejecting the authority behind the legislation, without challenging the authority to make binding laws.

The conclusion that autonomy of moral judgment is compatible with an internal attitude of acceptance and allegiance makes understandable the following kind of dilemma. One may regard particular laws as valid (duly enacted) and at the same time see them as embodying a morally intolerable policy. For example, to say that the expropriation laws of Nazi Germany were valid is compatible with refusing to obey such laws on moral grounds. In other circumstances, the internal attitude that law is valid is also compatible with general moral apathy.

Hart's analysis (and positivist theories generally) are intended to take no stand vis-à-vis the content of laws and therefore with regard to the moral character of laws. Of course, even a positivistic analysis may yield some conclusions about the inevitable content of laws. There are broad limits on what can within reason be made into law. Laws have to deal with present and future behavior; an intelligible law cannot order me to be two feet taller than I am nor can it command me to pay my taxes ten years before my birth. Laws must be addressed to persons. Commands issued to pebbles and waves will have little effect. But these practical limits are not moral limits. From the point of view of positivism, to say that duly enacted rules are for moral reasons not valid law is, according to Hart, to confuse the problem of identifying and defining law with the problem of evaluating and choosing laws. To say that a law is valid is to say something about its pedigree and nothing about its moral content (unless the rule of recognition itself involves a moral criterion for laws); it is clearly not an endorsement of the law. Nonetheless, Hart recognizes that morally repellent laws will erode general habits of obedience and change attitudes until the government is rejected and changed. The *validity* of each particular law can be independent of its moral qualities, but the *acceptability* of a system of primary and secondary rules will usually depend on its moral characteristics.

We can now see that Hart's account of the internal aspect of law is largely and intentionally negative. The existence of a legal system involves obeying rules neither exclusively out of fear nor exclusively out of moral conviction. Although both attitudes *may* be present, neither is the essential or defining characteristic of the internal aspect. What is essential is the disposition to see rules as emanating from a stable institutionalized authority and the expectation that others, like oneself, will use these rules in criticism and evaluation. It is important to notice that this is not a theory of motivation; theories that refer to fear or moral conviction are theories of motivation that tell us *why* persons obey the law. Hart's position is that there is no distinctive motivation for obedience but there is a distinctive attitude. His analysis of the concept of law does not seek to answer the question why people obey but only the question how they regard law. His advance over Austin and Kelsen is to show clearly that these are two quite separate questions.

Let's review some steps in the history of legal positivism. Austin's command theory picks out some of the most obvious and important formal features, but it is too broad. Kelsen takes seriously the distinction be-

tween power and authority, even if power is an in-
gredient of authority, and gives an account of law that
allows us to explain the continuity and self-limiting
character of some legal systems. These theoretical advances are consolidated and clarified by Hart. Continuity and change in legal systems are explained in terms
of the guiding role of secondary rules. The notion of
authority is explained by reference to the internal
aspect of legal rules. Having a clear idea of what positivists say and what questions they try to answer, we
must now face a larger problem. What can be said for
positivism in general as an approach to the concept
of law? Is law best explained by examining its formal
features?

Critics of Positivism; The Citizen and the Lawmaker

One way of criticizing positivism, and Hart as its most
sophisticated proponent, is by seeking how adequately
Hart answers his own questions; another is by asking
different questions. Joseph Raz takes the first approach
in his book, *The Concept of a Legal System.* He does not
disagree with positivism as a fruitful method. Nor does
he question the advances that Hart makes over Kelsen
and Austin in reviving philosophical debate about the
concept of law. He tries to build upon Hart's theory
both by refining it and by raising questions that he
thinks Hart failed to raise about the criteria for the
existence of a legal system and about the structure of
a legal system. I shall not discuss Raz's arguments in
any detail here but shall only try to give some sense
of the direction his thoughts take.[22]

Raz suggests, among other things, that the rule of
recognition is better seen as a fact than as a rule, namely
the fact that certain resources are taken as the sources

[22] Raz, *Concept,* Chapter 8.

of law. Further, he suggests that not only primary laws but the rule (or fact) of recognition may change over the life of a legal system. The legal system of the United States may come to have a different or much changed constitution and, arguably, remain the same legal system. In discussing questions of structure, Raz says that Hart's analysis is too simple; many kinds of rules are laws and yet are not included within the categories of primary rules (addressed to citizens, imposing obligations) and secondary rules (addressed to officials, instructing them in the use of their powers). Some laws specify permissions rather than impose duties, permissions addressed to ordinary citizens. Still other laws create exemptions from obligations, or impose obligations on officials, or delegate legislative power, and so on. It follows that the structure of a legal system is best understood by examining the complex internal relations of many different kinds of laws. Raz's book is an elaborate and generally successful attempt to do this.

A different approach to Hart is to ask questions about the concept of law that he leaves aside. To do this is to raise directly the question of the merits of positivism. Is it best to describe law by discussing its structure and other formal features? Hart, we have seen, considers the structure of law and not its content. We have seen qualifications of this, and further qualifications are needed. Hart admits that there are some universal features of human society and that all legal systems will be determined in their content by the need of societies to accommodate these conditions. These features are that persons are vulnerable to injury and death, that they are limited in their altruism, that they have approximately equal physical power, that there are limited economic resources, and that persons have limited understanding and will.[23] This is a modest concession with regard to content because Hart does not ask

[23] Hart, pp. 189-195.

whether certain universal goals, beyond these listed ac-
commodations, are inherent in man's self-understanding
and in the creation of legal systems.[24]

To put the point differently, Hart, in common with
other legal positivists, identifies law and describes it
largely by reference to formal features. He answers
the question of what the form of law is and is careful to keep this question apart from investigations of
what law ought to be, which is invariably a question
of content.

This distinction seems plausible enough. The question
of what law is does seem separate from the question
of what law ought to be. But this is not the end of the
matter. I shall try to show next that the question
"What is law?" can be asked from several different
points of view, that no point of view has inherent
priority over others, and that only from *some* points
of view are the questions separable. In other words,
there are points of view from which the formal positivist answer to the question "What is law?" is not
an adequate answer. I shall argue that a formal (positivist) analysis answers questions about the nature of
law that would be raised from the point of view of (a)
anyone who must treat the law as "given." It will not
be responsive to questions raised from the point of
view of (b) a decision-maker seeking guidance for the
determination of decisions in hard cases.

(a) Citizens treat the law as given when they have to
adapt their behavior to law, when they use their law-
given power to make enforceable wills and to incorporate, and so on. (Bear in mind that much legal work
has nothing to do with litigation.) The client or his
lawyer will determine the relevant law by implicitly

[24] Lon Fuller, in *The Morality of Law* (New Haven, 1963), argues that
there are other kinds of universal constraints on law that are derived
from the fact that a legal system must protect its own integrity and moral
force if it is to be self-sustaining.

using a rule of recognition (defining the resources that comprise law) and other secondary rules that determine how law is administered. A lawyer advising and representing a client will be concerned with the law as given and with research and prediction. When litigation occurs, the citizen and lawyer claim certain rights under existing law; ordinarily, they do not claim to be changing the law.[25] If we assume perfect enforcement, the laws of the state are unchangeable constraints on the citizen's actions, as unchangeable as laws of nature. In both cases the law says that particular actions will be followed by particular consequences.

(b) The judge in a hard case cannot simply treat the law as given. The formal characteristics of law as it is specify the form but not the substance of legal decisions. In particular, secondary rules will tell a judge what procedures to follow in rendering decisions but not what goals to pursue. The question whether the concept of law embodies goals will arise when we try to characterize law from the point of view of the judge rather than that of the client who receives law as given.

Although some tasks involve "mechanical jurisprudence," the direct application of rules to clear instances of violation, in other cases the judge has to use rules in situations in which the result is not predetermined. Hart calls these "penumbral" cases.[26] The language of legislation and of constitutions is in-

---

[25] It is probably a caricature of lawyers to say that they are "guns for hire" and are not concerned with moral judgments about the law as it stands and is likely to become. In fact the injustice of existing law is often an important argument in the lawyer's arsenal. And this is not only, or not always, mere lip service to an indefinitely malleable notion. The counterimage to the "gun for hire" is that of the lawyer working toward the realization of justice rather than working as a partisan. The theory of the adversary system is that these roles are reconcilable: the overall justice of the system is best served if the interests of clients are well served, if each side of each controversy has a full hearing. This is achieved by each lawyer acting as a partisan.

[26] Hart, pp. 121-132.

tentionally general, if not vague; judicial interpretation exists to fill these gaps. This is an inherent feature of law, because no legislator can ever anticipate and decide all the particular idiosyncratic cases that fall under a given law, can foresee the future and the questions it will pose. Moreover, not all creative judicial action is penumbral. Judges not only interpret general laws for specific cases but also change existing law by setting precedents for other cases. In doing so, they create new general rules.

In making "new law" courts usually say they are reconciling specific rules with more general rules. For example, the general formula used in Supreme Court decisions that change law in visible and sometimes revolutionary ways is that particular rules are changed to conform with the general rules of the Constitution. This marks the distinction between the functions of judges and legislators: judges exist to interpret and apply law, whereas legislators exist to make new law. I shall assume in what follows that judges in general act in good faith mindful of this distinction, that it is a distinction *de facto* as well as *de jure*. (This means that it is not simply a pretence and that the attempt to interpret the intent of legislators and of the framers of the Constitution is not word play but a real constraint.) If we do assume that judges apply existing law, what exactly is it that they apply and that constrains them?

As we shall see, Ronald Dworkin argues that Hart strongly implies that beyond a certain point nothing constrains them. When judges are working in a penumbral area of law, they have by definition exhausted the guidance that laws can give them. They may turn to other resources, and we may admire and criticize them for how they use those resources, but those resources are not law. It is interesting to look back once again at Austin and see how important this point was for him. Austin, like his contemporary and friend, John Stuart Mill, was a utilitarian who believed it was possible to measure objectively the moral value of various consequences of action. He thought that the quality of judicial decisions could clearly be improved if judges realized that they were free to employ utilitarian methods. Thus, it was of particular importance for him to develop a theory of law in which the law was limited to a sovereign's commands, and according to which a judge could *not* argue that he is bound to ignore utility because he is bound by various legal constraints other than the rules laid down for him to apply. This theme survives intact in Hart's theory.

In an influential critique of Hart, Dworkin takes up the debate at this point and claims that Hart's account of law is mistaken because law encompasses "standards that do not function as rules, but operate differently as principles, policies, and other sorts of standards."[27] Dworkin's point is about judges and not about legislators in this sense: although no one would contend that the various data that legislators are expected to take into account are part of the law (because law is the *result* of legislation, not its ingredients), one may well argue, as Dworkin does, that the constraints recognized by judges *are* part of the law.

Dworkin concedes that judges soon exhaust the relevant rules in hard cases. He agrees with the positivists that it is an illusion that the Constitution itself or other clear and compelling (primary or secondary) rules tell judges how to apply law in penumbral cases and how to change laws when, as in recent cases on racial discrimination, it is thought justifiable by the Court that laws be changed. It is equally an illusion, Dworkin continues, that there are no further constraints in

[27]Ronald Dworkin, "Is Law a System of Rules?," *Essays in Legal Philosophy*, Summers, ed. (Berkeley, 1968), p. 34.

these cases and that the decision depends "on the judge's own preferences amongst a sea of respectable extralegal standards, any one in principle eligible, because if that were the case we could not say that any rules were binding."[28] In short, Dworkin divorces the notion of law from the notion of a rule or system of rules. He suggests that in hard cases various principles that spell out binding constraints are recognized. Dworkin's examples usually spell out the implications of acting fairly; two such principles are that manufacturers in contracting with consumers must treat the consumer and the public interest fairly and that one party may not take unjust advantage of another.[29] Dworkin argues that these principles are part of the law even though they are not primary or secondary rules and even though they are not picked out by the rule of recognition.

What are the implications of this argument as I have represented it? It is evident that the argument is concerned with decision-making and not with the point of view of the citizen. The judge may claim, correctly or not, that fairness is an inherent feature of law, and the citizen may point without contradicting him to unfair laws and unfair administation. This is not a contradiction because the judge is not making an empirical claim. We can put this differently, in terms that are now familiar. To the extent that citizens have no power to change the law or shape it, they must treat the law as received, just as they must treat laws of nature. Judges treat law as an artifact to the extent that they have the power to shape it; to this extent it is *their* artifact. A conception of law that adequately represents the judge's point of view will raise questions about whether there is any inherent purpose to the institution of law, a purpose with enough clarity and specificity to guide

[28] Ibid., p. 51.
[29] Ibid., p. 36.

decision-making. I interpret Dworkin's argument accordingly: the principles that constrain decisions are not the personal preferences of the judge but something else, the purposes expressed in the principles that have shaped and motivated the collective creation of the legal system.

There are many more strands in Dworkin's critique of positivism and in his alternative theory. I shall consider them at many points in my discussion. Let's now, however, look at some interpretations and possible misinterpretations of this first strand. (a) When Dworkin says that law includes principles (and policies) as well as primary and secondary rules, is he saying (1) that each particular judge will be constrained and feel constrained by some principles or others, as well as by rules? Different judges may be constrained by different principles, but every judge will be constrained by *some* principles. This is not his point, as we can readily see. First, *this* view is that judges are constrained by principles of their own preference, whereas Dworkin invokes principles to show that petitioners are not to be at the mercy of a judge's own preferences. Second, Dworkin implies that a legal system is made up of primary rules, secondary rules, and principles; the principles can vary from judge to judge *no more* than the rules can so vary. Rules and principles are both constraints on decision.

Another interpretation is (2) that a particular legal system consists of specific rules and specific principles. In this view, Dworkin would be claiming that given principles are specific to a particular legal system and vary from system to system just as rules do. But Dworkin's examples suggest still a third interpretation whereby (3) certain principles (but not certain rules) transcend particular legal systems. The third view seems to fit some of Dworkin's examples, because he appeals to principles of fairness. Principles of fairness are not

restricted to particular systems in the way that rules
are. If fairness is to be identified with law at all, it seems
as if it ought to be identified with the concept of law:
every legal intervention in any legal system ought to
be fair. I conclude that some of Dworkin's principles
are intended to have this scope. Even this needs to be
qualified. The principle, if it is one, that enjoins judges
to be fair is so general and abstract that it is almost
empty of content. Judges who are bound by the injunction to be fair or to treat persons with equal respect
need to inform themselves about the concrete meaning
and content of these principles. To do so they will have
to look at the cultural and moral traditions of their
societies and at principles recognized and debated
through the history of their own legal tradition. Their
understanding of how to achieve fairness is not the
unpacking of a pure abstraction but the unpacking of
the abstraction in a context.

This view stands between (2) and (3). The principles
that bind a judge are not arbitrarily relative to particular legal systems because the guiding concepts—like
fairness and respect—are equally relevant as criteria for
evaluating any systems we might think about. But the
elaboration of those concepts is always in a particular
context where the judge is the inheritor and custodian
of a history of moral interpretation.

(b) Another problem of interpretation is this. Dwork-
kin can be read as supplementing Hart's analysis or as
offering a different and conflicting theory of law. It
would be superficial to say simply that for Hart "law
= rules" and for Dworkin "law = [rules and principles] "
and therefore their views conflict. We must go deeper.
The attempt to do so will clarify what questions each
philosopher is asking and at what points Hart's positivism is vulnerable to criticism.

Dworkin's formal analysis of the structure of a legal
system has two important differences from Hart's

analysis. The first point is that law includes rules *and principles* and the second is that principles are not picked out by the rule of recognition. In an article commenting on this difference, Joseph Raz says that Hart's use of the term *rule* is *equivalent* to Dworkin's use of the term *standard,* which embraces both rules and principles. Furthermore, if the rule of recognition includes the various constraints that judges say are incumbent on them and that appear as constraints in decisions as they are rendered, then the rule of recognition does indeed pick out principles as well as rules. In this way, Raz tries to defuse Dworkin's critique.[30]

Raz's criticism of Dworkin amounts to the claim that Dworkin and Hart are both offering formal accounts of the concept of law and that the accounts are largely interchangeable. This assumes that Dworkin is asking the same questions as Hart, looking at law as "given," and saying little about the guides for judges in hard cases. But it can be argued that Dworkin is not offering a formal account of law and that the question "What is law?" is not central to his concerns. What is central is the view that certain principles that have moral intent are binding and incumbent on judicial decision-makers, whether (as Dworkin holds) those principles are said to be part of law *or* whether they are not part of law but binding as part of public morality. This latter view is not touched by Raz's objections as I represent them here and embodies what Raz rejects as the "myth of common morality."[31] In other words, we must distinguish a formal thesis that says that principles are part of the law and that they are not picked out by the rule of recognition from a substantive thesis that says something about the source and nature

[30] Joseph Raz, "Legal Principles and the Limits of Law," *Yale Law Journal,* 81, 823, 832 (1972); Ronald Dworkin, "Social Rules and Legal Theory," *Yale Law Journal,* 81, 855 (1972).

[31] Raz, "Legal Principles," p. 850.

of those principles. The first thesis challenges Hart's answers; the second raises questions about content that Hart chooses not to raise at all.

It is evident from Raz's remark about the "myth of common morality" that he echoes the general positivistic rejection of that thesis, a posture especially evident in Kelsen. To the extent that Hart concurs, it is an important issue between himself and Dworkin. According to Hart, a discussion of the concept of law allows us to refer to the facts and procedures for change but not to the direction of change. He describes the track on which the race is run but says nothing about the direction of the race or the goals of the runners. Hart cautions us that a legal system is a legal system whether it becomes more or less just over time, and that its goals are indefinitely variable. In my interpretation, Dworkin is to be contrasted with Hart insofar as he claims that the attainment and implementation of certain principles are inherent in the law or the expectations surrounding it, whether or not these purposes are well or badly served.

Naturalism and Positivism

We can use Hart and Dworkin to represent two sides of a general debate that has been important throughout the history of legal philosophy. The debate is between naturalists, who claim that law is best explained by reference to natural moral principles, principles inherent in the notion of ideal society and the moral potentialities of persons, and positivists, who claim that law is best understood formally as a system of orders, commands, rules, and so forth, enforced by power. Positivists deny at least one of the following claims: (1) there is a natural moral order, (2) that natural moral order is accessible to human understanding, and (3) the concept of law must be understood by reference to a natural moral order. I shall briefly review the arguments on each side of the debate and show why the debate has continuing significance for the conduct of law.

According to naturalism in most of its forms, the ideal legal system is part of the blueprint of the ideal society. The ideal society, in turn, is one in which human perfectability and/or the constituents of happiness[32] are most fully realized. Any such Utopian theory implies that human nature is objectively knowable in the sense that we can extrapolate from general facts about misery and well-being (for example, from what we know about hunger, pain, health, and the need for security) to an adequate picture of the conditions of the good life for persons in general.[33] (In some theories the good life may be secured not for everyone, but for the majority or for the most deserving.)

Although it is possible to find the roots of this kind of theory in the works of Plato and Aquinas, it is characteristically an Enlightenment view. Utopia-making was a serious activity in the eighteenth century and human nature was a favorite object of "scientific" scrutiny by recourse to the methods and metaphors of natural science. Some legal systems, especially the Code Napoleon, represent the most ambitious application of this commitment to the creation of laws, laws that embody a vision of how people might live in perfect

[32] I am leaving out of consideration some religious or nonhumanist theories of the perfect society that put forth other goals than human well-being, broadly defined. Also, in referring to human goals as constituents of happiness, I am not claiming that happiness is the only or the primary good; I am using Aristotle's idea that happiness is the mark of having attained other human goals.

[33] I am ignoring theories that hold that law will be unnecessary in Utopia because there will be mutual benevolence. Some assumptions of this kind are made by Marx and Engels, as well as by B. F. Skinner in *Walden Two* (New York, 1948).

harmony, justice, and well-being, and most importantly of how law may be the vehicle for bringing this about.

Naturalism, then, presupposes that human nature, discoverable through investigation, is the source of law because law is to be the instrument for the realization of what is potential in human nature. A naturalistic theory is a theory that there is some natural order in which persons have a place, a natural order characterized by natural harmony. It presupposes that the point of humanly constructed laws is to emulate that natural order. Law as it is contains the seed of law as it ought to be.

The hinge on which such naturalist theories turn is the claim that human nature is knowable in the appropriate sense that enables us to construct Utopias and anticipate their laws. Positivist theories as a rule are instances of a general social philosophy that denies the possibility of this kind of knowledge. Of course, we know some universal facts about persons and their needs, pleasures, and potentialities. But what we know is limited, limited not because we do not have adequate tools but because adequate tools are inconceivable. Human nature and human capabilities, in this account, are not definable in this way and the very process of trying to understand human nature changes human nature by changing the conditions and context of human development.[34]

We can easily illustrate how far we have come from the comfortable conviction that law can be a blueprint for human perfection. Is it better to lead a reflective, scholarly life or an active life of public achievement? Is success in living to be measured in terms of contentment, stimulation, or achievement? Is knowledge good

---

[34] For several perspectives on the differences between scientific and social explanation (or rather between explanation in natural sciences and social sciences) see the essays in Alan Ryan, ed., *The Philosophy of Social Explanation* (Oxford, 1973).

in itself, worth achieving in itself? All these questions, which philosophers from Aristotle through Rousseau tried to answer, seem to us almost unanswerable. We are more aware than persons have ever been of human diversity and of the fact that one may not be able to anticipate one's own satisfactions much less those of others. We think a straightforward answer to any of these questions will merely express a personal preference and create the risk that it will be imposed on others in violation of their own right to choose what they will be and do.

Another difference between the theory types of naturalism and positivism can be seen in their treatment of the distinction between means and ends. It is easy for a naturalist to draw the distinction: well-being is the end; political activity and the construction and use of laws are among the means. For other naturalists, like Aristotle, well-being is realized in and through political activity; the means and ends are not separated in time because living well is a process and not simply a goal.[35] A positivist, on the other hand, will refrain from speaking of means to well-being because he believes that little can be said about well-being in a general way beyond, for example, Hart's account of the minimal demands of social existence.

It follows that the projects of constructing Utopias and emulating natural law lose their sense and justification. The makers of law must be more modest in their goals and ambitions. One application of this view occurs when John Stuart Mill concludes in "On Liberty" that the state is not justified in making positive interventions, imposing a certain person's conception of the good life on others; the state should intervene only to prevent harm of one person by another. Free interchange of ideas in the exercise of liberty is urged,

---

[35] Aristotle, *Nicomachean Ethics, passim.*

because there is no "scientific" way to discover the truth of human well-being. It is a short step from this to the view that the process of self-discovery in general *is* the good life.[36]

The conception of law that follows from this kind of theory is a relatively modest and "realistic" one. It is the view that laws, as coercive social rules, have represented many kinds of purposes and have been used to achieve many sorts of goals. They have been used in the interests of the governed and they have also been used to frustrate these ends. Laws are *posited* by authoritative decision-makers and no particular goals and interests are to be identified with the concept of law. We have seen that Austin, Kelsen, Hart, and Raz are positivists of various kinds.

Obviously, a contemporary naturalist can hardly deny human diversity and can hardly put forth an uncontroversial account of the best way to live. He can, however, make a more modest claim that is the basis of a more modest naturalism. The claim has two parts. First, the naturalist says that even if we are aware that human aspirations are diverse, we are also aware that some ways of living are clearly preferable to others. A life in which one has choice over career and social relationships and the means to carry out choices is preferable to a less privileged life. Health and security are preferable to illness and vulnerability. In saying this, the naturalist is borrowing and extending Hart's list of natural conditions. The second part of the claim is that we know that the liberty to have varied experiences and to choose knowledgeably among ways of living has

---

[36] This second kind of theory links empiricism, as in the work of J. S. Mill, to existentialism, which affirms that persons make their own nature. All of these theories share with Kant the conviction that persons are capable of moral and legal responsibility only because they, alone among creatures, can set rules for themselves and obey them. They are not determined in their behavior by given needs and goals.

great value in itself and that an essential purpose of the state and government is to maximize and safeguard such liberty. Thus, paradoxically, the admission of what we do *not* know about human nature yields a naturalistic goal for society, a goal to be embodied in law.

Contemporary naturalists like Dworkin are careful to avoid the pitfalls of eighteenth-century thinkers and do not claim to offer a blueprint for Utopia.[37] Dworkin, for example, claims only that we can identify certain moral commitments that are pervasive in our legal system and that are expressed in terms of inherent inalienable rights; the principles implemented in proper decisions set forth these rights. Thus the debate between positivism and naturalism in our own day is often not between the friends and enemies of liberties. The question is rather whether liberty is to be defended by recourse to a theory of natural rights and whether assumptions about such rights inhere in the concept of law.

I shall now summarize this section and retrace the complicated debate between positivists and naturalists. The essential claim in each case is elusive. Hart reminds his readers that the label "positivism" covers many confusions and ideas.[38] Among the theses that have come to be identified with positivism are the following ones. (1) "Laws are the commands of human beings." Austin would agree; Hart would argue that secondary rules, although made by persons, are not to be seen as commands. (2) "There is no necessary connection between law and morals, or law as it is and law as it ought to be." This is Hart's view and it is distinctive of positivism in all its forms. I shall have more to say

---

[37]Skinner is a counterexample. See also his *Beyond Freedom and Dignity* (New York, 1972). I am leaving out of account many kinds of naturalistic theories, in particular Marxist theories.

[38]Hart lists these five accounts of positivism at p. 253, *Concept of Law.*

about it. (3) "The analysis of the meaning of legal concepts is to be distinguished from historical and sociological inquiries, and the critical appraisal of law in terms of social aims, morals, etc." Here there is a difference of opinion. Hart is comfortable with this distinction, whereas a theorist like Dworkin would probably argue that *some* "aims" are to be identified with the concept of law, while others may arbitrarily come to characterize some legal systems and not others. (4) "A legal system is one in which correct decisions can be deduced from predetermined legal rules by logical means alone." There is no suggestion in Austin, Kelsen, or Hart that this is so. Laws require interpretation and application to situations that were not anticipated by the legislators. (5) "Moral judgments cannot be established, as statements of fact can, by evidence, proof, or rational arguments." This last thesis is not explicitly discussed by most legal positivists. As Raz's observation about the "myth of common morality" shows, the thesis is implicit in their approach.

Consider the following ramifications of the fifth thesis. We have seen that positivists say there must be a clear distinction between law as it is and law as it ought to be, roughly reflecting the citizen's standpoint toward law as something given. Definition (2) of positivism is uncontroversial in this respect if it says that there is no necessary connection between the laws that exist and the laws that we desire, or that we regard as best. But the limitation of positivism is that it fails to notice that this is not the same thing as saying that there is no necessary connection between the concepts of law and justice. In other words, the concept of law may refer not only to a fact (the existence of coercive rules) but also to an ideal (the use of such rules to achieve moral goals and well-being). The underlying philosophical point is that positivism is ordinarily associated with a strict separation between so-called facts and values and between statements about law as it is and law as it ought to be. As I argued earlier in this chapter, this works well for such claims as "The law requires two witnesses for a will to be enforceable" (a fact) and for "The tax law ought not to impose any liability on persons earning less than $5,000" (a value). It is not an exhaustive dichotomy if we talk about *law* instead of *laws* and say "Law involves the fair disposition of petitioners' claims" or (the same proposition) "Petitioners' claims ought to be disposed of fairly." In either version the claim is not an empirical fact nor an expression of personal preference; it purports to be a conceptual fact of the kind discovered in conceptual analysis.[39]

What does this have to do with the debate between positivists and naturalists? First, the dichotomy between facts and values can mislead those who accept it naively into claiming that no factual propositions can specify norms of judgment. But obviously conceptual descriptions (facts about concepts) like "Cars are designed and used for driving" state a basis for judging cars. Positivism tends to be identified with the mistake that claims about law as a concept cannot state a basis for judging laws and legal systems. Second, while a positivist like Hart is sensitive to the nature of conceptual analysis, he suggests implicitly that the concept "law" is unlike such concepts as "car" or "knife" in just this respect: no general goals can be identified with the concept of law and determine its content, except in a minimal sense.[40] Knives in general have a point (pun unintended); legal systems do not. Third, naturalists extend the analysis of artifacts like cars and knives to

---

[39] Again we can compare statements about knives that illustrate the same point: (a) a fact: "This knife has a blue handle," (b) a value: "This knife ought to be able to cut rubber," and (c) a conceptual fact: "Knives are for cutting" or "Knives ought to cut."

[40] See note 23.

the analysis of law insofar as they say that the concept of law generates guiding principles for judgment because the concept of human nature is rich enough to generate some universal social goals. Liberty is an example of such a goal.

Practices, Open and Closed

In the background of our analysis of the structure of a legal system lies an obvious analogy, which is particularly appealing to positivists. Legal systems, it is said, have much in common with games. Legal systems and games are both practices; a practice is "any form of activity specified by rules . . . which give the activity its structure."[41] The rules not only give the activity its structure from the standpoint of an external observer, who will describe the practice by describing its rules, but also for the participants, who use the rules as standards to guide them in acting and in criticizing the actions of others.

Let's see where this comparison leads. If we are interested in the goals of players of games, we must look to the rules of the game that tell players their object. The goal, in turn, determines strategy. In baseball it is to score the most runs and in chess it is to checkmate the opponent's king. Similarly, the purpose of a practice that is not a game, like law, may be specified in the rules, just as the Preamble to the Constitution of the United States sets forth purposes to be achieved. Just as the purposes of a game are intrinsic to the rules, the purposes of a legal system are intrinsic to that particular system and are to be found, if anywhere, in its primary and secondary rules as documented by

[41] John Rawls, "Two Concepts of Rules," *Philosophical Review,* 64, 3, n. 1 (1955).

constitutions or statutes. We thus arrive by a different route at a conclusion that parallels Hart's claim that he has offered an exhaustive account of the concept of law in his appeal to the notion of law as the conjunction of various kinds of rules; principles and goals, if they are part of law, will be found in the rules and standards of the particular system by resort to a rule of recognition.

In summary, the notion of a game is used to typify any shared activity in which persons collectively are governed by rules. There are all kinds of games played for all kinds of purposes: games for pleasure, games to acquire skills, and games (like war games) to test strategy. A set of laws is like a game played publicly with general rules enforced by authority. Legal systems, like games, have various purposes: the security of the sovereign, the welfare of the governed, and so on. The structure of law and the supposed arbitrariness of its rules are thus made clear by the seductive analogy of games. Positivists use it to buttress their analysis. They will conclude that at best there are purposes of particular legal systems, as there are of particular games, but there is no purpose of law.

How persuasive is the comparison? Are legal systems sufficiently like games for us to learn something about the structure of legal systems by thinking about games? And do legal systems as a group, like games as a group, lack a purpose that is distinctive of the very notion of a legal system?

Note that one might claim that games as a group *do* have purposes that are distinctive of the notion of a game. Thus one might say that the purpose of players as set down in the rules of baseball, e.g., to score more runs than the opposing team, are to be distinguished from the purposes of the institution of a game—to give pleasure, to cultivate skills, and so on. Just as these purposes are not to be confused with the purposes set

down in the rules of baseball or chess, the general purposes of law and legal systems are not to be found in
the rules of particular legal systems.

This analogy is only partially helpful because it con-
ceals an important distinction. The purpose or point
of law that a naturalist like Dworkin is after is indeed
outside the rules (he would claim), but at the same
time it is something that guides decision-makers (judges)
in their relevant moves as "players." But that is just
what the alleged purposes of baseball do *not* do. It is
not open to an umpire to justify a call of "safe" by
saying that keeping Jones in the game will earn more
money for the home team, and it is not open to a
batter to demand a fourth strike so that he may better
cultivate skill.

This criticism suggests that there are fatal flaws in a
theory that takes games as the paradigm of practices
in general and interprets law accordingly. To see why
this is so, we must distinguish between two kinds of
practices, which I shall call open and closed practices.

Games like baseball and chess are typically closed
practices. This means they have all the following features. The participants are typically in adversary roles.
The rules define more or less exhaustively the functions
a participant can have and the moves he or she can
make, as well as the goals of the players. Instances of
a game have explicit beginnings and ends, and there is
no procedure for changing the rules during play. Moves
are discrete, and each player has a finite and clearly
demarcated set of options for each move. Each player
is expected to know the rules and abide by them. Most
importantly of all, players cannot justify their actions
by appeal to purposes not set forth in the rules. John
Rawls makes this point when he says that a player *qua*
player can have no authority to question

the propriety of following a rule in particular cases.
To engage in a practice, to perform those actions

specified by a practice, *means* to follow the appropriate rules. If one wants to do an action which a certain practice specifies then there is no way to do it except to follow the rules which define it. Therefore, it doesn't *make sense* for a person to raise the question whether or not a rule of a practice correctly applies to *his* case where the action he contemplates is a form of action defined by the practice. If someone were to raise such a question, he would simply show that he didn't understand the situation in which he was acting.[42]

Rawls's point involves an appropriate description of most closed practices, like most games. The effectiveness of playing a game depends on closure, on the fact that a player ordinarily cannot raise the question whether a rule applies to his case. He cannot, in other words, appeal to principles or shared goals in asking to have a rule waived. The rules anticipate all situations; in baseball, for example, situations do not arise in which it is unclear whether or not a player ought to have four strikes. This is related to the fact that rules of closed practices do not have what Hart calls "open texture,"[43] the intentional generality of laws that allows them to be interpreted for unanticipated and unforeseeable situations.

These essential features of closed practices are not present in all practices. I shall call a practice that lacks them an "open" practice. Legal systems are examples. Participants are not adversaries until and unless they violate rules. Participation is open ended; laws, for example, apply to persons night and day in an indeterminate number of ways. It is ordinarily impossible to give an exhaustive and complete account of an open practice because the rules evolve continually.

---

[42] Ibid., p. 26.
[43] Hart, pp. 120–132.

(Examples of open practices are particular languages as well as particular legal systems.)

The most important consequence of the distinction between open and closed practices is that moves are *under*determined by rules in an open practice. This means that authoritative decisions in cases of conflict must be made with an eye to something beyond the rules, the purposes and goals of the practice. The decisions of judges are not fully determined by rules. In hard cases, where the rules have open texture, judges will have recourse to principles that represent values. Moreover, petitioners in hard cases will make claims by appealing to such values and citing such principles. A defendant in a tax case may argue that it would work an undue hardship on businessmen in his position to construe an ambiguous tax statute in a particular way. Or a poor criminal may argue that the due process clause of the fourteenth amendment to the Constitution entitles him or her to have counsel assigned as soon as he or she is charged with a crime. As players in the practice, the role of such defendants will be markedly different from that of baseball or chess players, whose moves are fully determined by rule and strategy. In other words, in an open practice, the goals of the practice may be summoned to justify or question a particular move. (This is a feature of such open practices as languages as well as legal systems; a move that violates rules of grammar can always be justified by "You understood me, didn't you?")

A theorist who compares law to a game will analyze it, as positivists like Hart do, in terms of its constituent rules. But to analyze law as if it were a closed practice is to see it as an oddly defective one insofar as its rules have open texture and therefore generate hard cases. Thus, special technicians (judges) have to be called in to repair the machinery when it breaks down. Judges are ordinarily not needed in chess. On the other hand, to see law as an open practice is to move away from seeing it as a defective game. It is to describe it, we have seen, not as if the rules of law are given to the citizen as the rules of chess are given to a player, but from the perspective of the shaper of a coordinate activity who has and uses a conception of the goals and purposes that inform the rules and determine change.

A positivist like Hart is able to distinguish *in part* between games and open practices by recourse to secondary rules, rules that (among other things) describe procedures for change. These rules specify the *how* rather than the *why* of change. The stand off between the positivist and the naturalist takes this form: the positivist persists in holding that practices are exhausted by (or adequately characterized in terms of) a specification of their rules. He concedes that he cannot prove the case for *law* affirmatively by demonstrating that *games* are characterized in terms of rules; he concedes that legal systems are not entirely like games. On the other hand, the positivist argues the case negatively by saying that there is no universal purpose or shared goal of the cooperative enterprise that is a legal system; and, if this is so, we cannot point to a universal *why* for all change in laws. The burden is on the naturalist to convince us that there are such principles and that they are universal.

Toward a Theory of Decision-Making

Dworkin reads and criticizes Hart's model of rules *as* a theory about decision-making.[44] He offers his own account of judicial discretion and of the constraints of proper decisions.

We distort the debate if we see it simply as a debate

---

[44] Dworkin, op. cit.

about the merits of particular definitions of law, definitions that claim to be exhaustive. Rather, there are
various questions about the concept, various perspectives from which different questions seem important.
"What is law from the standpoint of the subject?"
The subject will look for duly authorized rules that
define obligations. "What is law from the point of
view of the judge?" The judge will seek guidance in
deciding hard cases.

It is important to see that much agreement exists
among these several analyses. It is uncontroversial that
law is to be characterized partly in terms of the internal
relations of different kinds of standards and that the
existence of particular laws is tied to the notion of
validity or *formal* legitimacy. It is also uncontroversial
that judges do not do their job properly if they decide
cases by appeal to personal taste and whim. But the
controversy is real and important. It is in large part a
debate about the analysis of decision-making. What
are the constraints on judges? Do they include universal
principles of fairness and justice? If so, are they derived
from the rights of persons? Or do they have a different
basis? It is a characteristic naturalist stance to answer
such questions by defending a theory of human nature
and a theory of rights. I shall look at these questions in
the next chapter.

2

Judicial

Decisions

•

Positivism and Decision-Making

Near the beginning of Chapter 1, I introduced the example of a hypothetical court, much like the United States Supreme Court, deciding a constitutional case about representation of counsel. One point of the example is to show how little the judges agree about how their job ought to be done. They disagree about whether laws ought to be applied as "mechanically" as possible. They have varying opinions about what part, if any, moral opinions and moral arguments ought to play in their decisions. And they certainly have diverse views about what it would mean to use moral considerations, about what moral resources exist for them to use.

Our hypothetical example is not fiction. Judicial decision-making is not just a topic of mystery and controversy for philosophers of law to ponder in class-rooms and journal articles. It is a topic about which judges and lawyers themselves have all sorts of views. My purpose here is to look at some of the more plausible and interesting ways in which these questions can be answered. Theories about the nature of law are also, in many cases, theories about judging and theories about the relation of morality to legal decisions. We have already seen that some positivists aspire to say something informative and useful about all these issues.

Positivism has some obvious consequences for the analysis of decision-making. If (a) law consists only of rules that satisfy certain formal conditions, and if (b) a judge is constrained in decision-making only by what is law, then (c) a judge is not constrained by principles, substantive moral norms, and so forth, as long as they do not satisfy the formal conditions that define and limit what is law. If, on the other hand, law in its essence consists not only of rules but also of moral principles (which, for example, may describe the rights of persons) and if the judge is constrained by law, then judges are constrained by principles that in some sense are substantive moral norms. This second view is similar to the alternative posed by Dworkin to the theory of decision-making that, he says, is implicit in Hart.[1] Hart *does* say that judges in hard cases (cases that are not clearly and easily decided by existing rules, primary and secondary) have "discretion"; because their decisions are not determined by existing rules, they will be guided by "extralegal" considerations.[2] According to Dworkin, this is to say that there is nothing in *law* to constrain a judge from acting to implement his own preferences and there is no basis

[1] Ronald Dworkin, *Taking Rights Seriously* (Cambridge, 1977), Chapter 2. Dworkin's book contains most of his previous work in philosophy of law, including "The Model of Rules." See Chapter 1, notes 27 and 30.
[2] Hart, *Concept,* Chapter VII, Section 3.

within that which is *law* on which to criticize a judge
for doing so. Dworkin concludes that this is a good
reason for thinking positivism is a defective theory of
judicial decision-making.

The two points about positivism that need interest us
now are the views that positivism offers an account
of the essence of law and that law and only law is what
constrains the judge in decision-making. Let's recon-
sider both views. At several points in Chapter 1 I implied that the first point is an attempt to answer an
unanswerable question, unanswerable because it is
not one but many questions.[3] Before trying to answer
the question, "What is law?" (or "What is the essence
of law?"), we must examine it and see that it conflates
several different real questions about law in different
contexts. For example, in the context of completing
my tax forms, I look to the primary rules[4] that govern
my relevant behavior. We saw that Hart's theory offers
a sensible account of the criterion that I use in this
context, or that a client or lawyer will use in many
familiar situations. But if I am a judge, I will run out
of primary rules in hard cases; that's what is distinctive
of a hard case. Even if I am not a judge, but an armchair
critic of the Nuremberg trials, for example, the positivist's remarks will be relevant, but of limited relevance.
They will show me in what way it makes sense to say
that the iniquitous rules governing (for example) the
administration of concentration camps in Germany
during the Second World War were legal, but they will
not show me why, from a different point of view,
one is tempted to withhold the label. ("Such practices
cannot be law!") The positivist would surely be correct
in saying that this judgment raises conceptual questions

[3]Compare Ludwig Wittgenstein, *Philosophical Investigations* (Oxford,
1953), Section 593 and *passim*.

[4]I shall use Hart's terminology when the notions are intuitively clear
and relatively independent of his theory.

that differ from those raised by the hypothetical client. But these are all questions about the concepts of law, legal obligation, and so on, as seen from various points of view in various contexts.

Just as "What is the essence of law?" conflates many different questions, "What is the essence of judicial decision-making?" is a question that conflates various problems. Among these problems are questions about the logical constraints on decision-making (a judicial decision cannot contradict itself), questions about practical possibility and impossibility (a decision must be such that it can *in practice* be carried out[5]), questions about the role of existing primary and secondary rules in shaping the substance of future decisions, questions about the scope of discretion of judges in hard and easy cases alike, questions about the resources judges *in fact* use to decide hard cases, questions about the resources judges *ought* to use to decide hard cases, questions about the resources of critics in evaluating what judges do, and so on. Of course, these issues are interdependent, but the relations among them are complex.

The second point that needs critical scrutiny is the assumption that only what is defined as law constrains the judge as decision-maker, that if law is defined as the union of primary and secondary rules, then these rules are the only constraints on decision. It is easy to see that this conclusion would seem very persuasive to a theorist who is preoccupied with the metaphor of games.[6] In a game involving adversaries, what is not forbidden is permitted and forms part of a usable and ordinarily useful strategy. Players are constrained from using certain means to win by rules forbidding their use. There may be a more-or-less strict division between what adversary moves are allowable and what ones are

[5] Lon Fuller, in *The Morality of Law,* traces the substantive implications of such practical constraints on the structure of legal systems.

[6] See Chapter 1, pages 46–51.

not allowable and therefore criticizable.[7] Even when we say that players ought to play fairly and not just follow the rules, the pressures of adversary play will have the result that fairness will be translated into additional explicit rules.

This kind of translation does not occur when we are dealing with practices that are not inherently adversary and competitive, like the family or the institutions of education, or with persons, like judges, whose institutional role is not that of adversaries. (In other words, the translation occurs readily in what I have called closed practices but not in open practices.) Why is this so? If we consider such institutions as the family or the institutions of education, it is not plausible to think that roles and responsibilities are simply exhausted by the rules of the enterprise, and that what is not forbidden is therefore allowed and exempt from the criticism that it is a dereliction of responsibility.

A parent or teacher is expected to pursue shared and altruistic purposes and not expected to defeat an "opponent" by all available means. A teacher who merely plays by the set rules of employment has barely begun to do his or her job. The same, I shall try to show, can be said of judges. Thus, although certain procedural rules of law (Hart's secondary rules) do constrain judges, they are only the most general and formal bases for analyzing judicial decision.

So far I have looked at two reasons for questioning positivism as a theory of judicial decision. First, I suggested that those who are looking for the essence of law may best be reinterpreted and seen to ask more modest questions about law from particular points of view. Second, I questioned whether a definition of law

[7]Criticizable, that is, as a violation of rules. A move in a game may also be criticized as poor strategy or as unfair. These are not counterexamples to the claim that, in games, what is not forbidden is allowed. Poor strategy is allowed and not forbidden; unfairness is implicitly forbidden and not allowed.

in terms of the rules of law must necessarily be taken
as a definition of the constraints on judicial decision
and of the criteria of criticism.

Whatever may have been the intentions of various
positivists, it is clear that there are alternatives to the
view that judges are constrained only by legal rules
and that a definition of law is *per se* an account of
the constraints on judicial decision. A fresh way of making the point is this. Let's say that a belief in "natural
morality" is a belief that some moral goals are universal
because they enjoin the satisfaction of universal human
needs or desires. A belief in "positive morality" is, in
contrast, a belief that all moral norms are social conventions for behavior and for the criticism of behavior,
and they do not express natural or universal features
of persons and experience. A legal positivist may have
any one of three views about judicial decision. It is
compatible with legal positivism as the quest for a
definition of law that a positivist *may* hold that a judge
who judges correctly is constrained in decision-making
by the rules of law alone *or* by the rules of law and
by natural morality *or* by the rules of law and by
positive morality. Kelsen seems to be a positivist of the
first kind,[8] Austin and John Stuart Mill are positivists
of the second kind,[9] and the Scandinavian philosopher
Alf Ross is a positivist of the third kind.[10] To the extent that Hart recognizes in law some minimal incorpo-
ration of universal constraints of human existence and
regards judges as doing their job properly in shaping
law to meet these constraints, he seems to align himself in a moderate way with Austin and Mill.[11]

The point of this section is a cautionary one. It is

[8] Kelsen, *General Theory*, pp. 20–21, 410–411.
[9] Austin and Mill, following Bentham, commend utilitarian principles
of decision-making. Any utilitarian theory presupposes a natural standard
for determining utility. See Mill, *Utilitarianism* (various editions) and
Austin, *Province*, pp. 37–40, 73, 112, 180–183.
[10] Alf Ross, *On Law and Justice* (Berkeley, 1959).
[11] Hart, *Concept*, Chapter IX, Section 2 (discussed in Chapter 1).

generally unhelpful to look for views about sound decision-making by looking at debates about positivism. This is because the aims of positivism are themselves variable and because many positivistic theories entail no particular answers to the question, "What constrains judges?" One reason for this is that the question is obviously ambiguous. It may be a question about what is *permissible* in judging or about what is *desirable;* many ways of proceeding may be permissible without being desirable. Another ambiguity is whether it is a question in pursuit of a *description* of what constrains judges or one seeking a criterion for what counts as *justification* of a judicial decision. In the next section I shall explain these distinctions and why they have often been ignored both by natural law theorists and by so-called legal realists.

Natural Law and Legal Realism:
Two Theories of Decision

There are several points of view from which decision-making becomes disarmingly simple to characterize. We saw in Chapter 1 that some theories of natural law say that natural law exists as a blueprint for ideal social organization against which the laws of men are to be measured. Natural law may have any of several sources, for example, human nature or the revealed word of a deity. (An appeal to natural law may or may not be intuitionistic. This means that a proponent of natural law may appeal to *public* evidence of natural law or he may claim that he intuits the rules and that appeal to evidence is irrelevant.)

There are both weak and strong theories of natural law. A theory is what I shall call a weak theory of natural law if it says that there are some substantive boundaries on judicial decision. For example, we saw that Hart points out that any judge will know that material resources are relatively scarce in comparison with what would comfortably satisfy all human wants. Thus, a feature of any decision is that the petitioner's claims be evaluated with attention to this fact, that limited resources constrain the achievement of goals. This is a weak theory of natural law, because natural facts of this kind give little guidance in hard cases and are compatible with many kinds of decisions, some of which may seem to us fair and sensible, others of which may seem outrageous. We have said very little about decision-making when we have uncovered such facts. It is appropriate to say that a weak theory of natural law like Hart's makes reference to facts about the general *functions* of law but not to specific *goals*. It is a function of law to provide for the allocation of natural resources, but it would be a goal of law to achieve a particular kind of allocation.

A strong theory of natural law, on the other hand, says that natural principles or goals for law are available to judges and entail particular decisions in hard cases. An example of a set of principles of this kind would be a complex moral or religious code. We shall see shortly that a code that anticipates and gives clear solutions for *all* situations that may come before a judge may be inconceivable. An example of a theory that may entail decisions in at least some hard cases is one put forward by John Rawls. Rawls derives and defends principles of justice that generally apply in societies that have attained a certain minimal level of material well-being. For example, the following principle is said to be part of the concept of justice: "Bring about the most extensive liberty for each person which is compatible with a like liberty for all."[12] Rawls may concede that his is only a relatively strong theory and that it does not entail a decision in all hard cases.

[12] John Rawls, *A Theory of Justice* (Cambridge, 1971), Chapter II, Section 11.

But it does give much more guidance than Hart's theory. For example, it tells us that such liberties as free speech and equal opportunity in employment cannot be compromised just because the economic cost of protecting these exercises of liberties is great. It also tells us that persons have an equal right to be considered in the distribution of material goods. These principles need to be interpreted in particular contexts, and judges may well disagree about how they are to be realized. At the same time, they place clear substantive limits on what counts as a decision justifiable as just. Another example of a relatively strong theory is one that posits a universal goal like the satisfaction of human wants or the realization of human capacities or the satisfaction of human needs and then claims to offer a universal account of wants, capacities or needs. As we saw in Chapter 1, it is scarcely plausible that such an account can be produced at the level of specificity that solves all hard cases for judges. It is one thing to say that there are universal rights to minimal education, shelter, protection, and so forth. It is something quite different to say that all hard cases can be resolved by resorting to such an account of universal rights.[13]

A strong theory of natural law assumes, of course, not only that decisive principles or goals exist but that judges can find them. It would be a silly theory to say

[13] It is a relevant matter of philosophical controversy whether so-called facts and values can be bridged in this way. Are there any facts about experience, human nature, transcendental beings, and so on, from which it follows that certain actions are to be done? The implication here has to be weaker than logical entailment. An example of a weaker implication is the claim that the fact that x is beneficial is a good reason for doing x and will therefore arouse the expectation that x will be done; the failure to do x will not "make sense" in the absence of a countervailing reason. One must be careful to distinguish facts that are *always* good reasons (but may be overridden by better reasons) from facts that are *sometimes* good reasons. An example of the latter is the reason, x is desired by persons. Benefit is always a good, but may sometimes be overridden by other goods; satisfaction of desires is often but not always a good. The moral prescription to benefit others is thus uncontroversial in a way in which the prescription to satisfy their desires is not.

that there *are* bases for decision but they are altogether inaccessible to the minds of judges or their critics. In a strong theory, the judge's role is to apply the relevant deciding norms. But this must not be confused with the view that judging is easy or that anyone can do it. Uncovering and understanding the relevant norms may involve special expertise, training, or sensitivity. Good judges may be rare; but the theory is that even when a correct decision is hard to determine, there *is* a correct decision and the sole job of the judge is to find it.

It is obvious that with any really strong theory many hard questions disappear. For one thing, there is no need to distinguish between what is permissible and what is desirable for a judge to do. The job of the judge is to find the right answer and anything else is an inadequate performance. There is no range of permissible alternatives, some better than others. For another thing, the description of what a judge does is simplified. The job is simply to apply the definitive principles of decisions. Accordingly, there is no separate question about what counts as justification, since a decision made in accord with the determinative resources for decisions is obviously justified. To summarize, there is little that is problematic about judicial decision-making for a theorist who holds that there is natural law in the strong sense and that natural law is accessible to judges.

A strong theory of natural law is a theory about a decision procedure for hard cases. Note, however, that one may claim that there is a decision procedure for judging without claiming that there is natural law. A positivist, for example, *may* say that there is some posited and arbitrary set of rules set for the particular legal system that is sufficiently precise to determine the correct answer for all cases. It is the business of judges, in this view, to apply the rules and not to look beyond them. An example is the claim that in determining the constitutionality of a piece of legislation, an American judge need simply lay it against the Constitution and observe whether it fits.[14] Such a claim illustrates a theory of mechanical jurisprudence (Hart's label).

There are relatively weak versions of such a theory and here I am concerned only with the strong version which posits a decision procedure. The weak version is that a constitution (or other ultimate rules of the system) sets general boundaries for permissible decisions. Within these bounds judges may decide cases variously, but they have no power to alter the boundary rules. Such rules may specify and limit the kinds of considerations which judges may take into account in deciding. For example, a rule may direct judges to find criminal guilt or innocence without looking into the mental condition of those accused of crime. It may direct them to ignore mental condition in imposing punishments. Another example is that judges may or may not be told to take corporate intentions into account in deciding whether antitrust laws have been violated. These guidelines still allow judges to disagree about many factors, and they allow much variation in decisions. In the strong version, on the other hand, the rules allow no variability. Strong theories, as we have seen, make decision-making unproblematic. They focus attention on the principles or goals that are the definitive resources of decision and not on the agents or methods of their application.

We must now investigate how and why strong theories fail. First of all, a strong natural law theory must account for the sources of natural law and for its legitimacy. If we have a theory that says natural law

[14] Cf. the majority opinion of the Supreme Court in *United States* v. *Butler,* 297 U.S. 1 (1936), in which Justice Roberts says, "When an act of Congress is appropriately challenged in the courts as nonconforming to the judicial mandate the judicial branch of the Government has only one duty—to lay the article of the Constitution which is invoked beside the statute which is challenged and to decide whether the latter squares with the former."

has a transcendental source (the word of God, for example), access to the source depends on sharing some ultimate faith or conviction. When this appeal is intuitive or emotive, there are no mutually shared rational procedures that a believer can use to convert a nonbeliever or by which a nonbeliever can participate in the intuitions. (A believer may, of course, persuade nonbelievers to accept and follow his procedures for pragmatic reasons.)[15] When natural law lacks this sort of basis, it ordinarily derives social goals from an understanding of the nature of things—of persons, of society, or of human aspirations or needs. The difficulty facing any argument of *this* kind is one which we already met in Chapter 1. Although we can say enough about human nature and conditions of life to set minimal substantive conditions for any legal system, these will involve very general goals.[16] A hard case will, by definition, be one about which reasonable persons may well differ, a case in which certain reasonable and important goals may pull a conscientious judge in one direction and other goals in the opposite direction. The assumption that the investigation of human nature will yield rules to make all hard cases uncontroversial, if not easy, is itself an act of faith to which experience gives little support.[17] What kind of knowledge about human nature or the world will make it *easy* for a judge to decide

[15] In other words, a nonbeliever may be persuaded to pretend to share the believer's practices because doing so will maintain public order, or because it will keep him in power, and so on.

[16] Again, cf. Hart, *Concept,* Chapter IX, Section 2.

[17] This issue involves intimidatingly large questions. Given the present state of psychology, sociology, and anthropology, it would be rash to claim that our knowledge of human nature tends toward universal laws of behavior or of experience. We discover both uniformities and diversity; both sorts of discoveries are sometimes unexpected. But even if we discovered greater and greater uniformity, even if we aspired in social science to the kind of universality claimed for physical science, these uniformities would not be uniformities in human wants, needs, or satisfactions. Surely social science, in showing the complexity and diversity of personal and social experience, shows that such expectations are naive.

whether to allow a zoning exemption for the construction of a needed power plant in the face of strong opposition from local residents who argue correctly that the plant will adversely affect their farming community? What kind of knowledge will determine whether abortion ought to be forbidden or whether a woman has the right to decide what happens to her body, at least in the early months of pregnancy? Of course, investigations of various kinds will be relevant, and a good judge will find out as much as possible. But no amount of information will take away the intractability of some problems of these kinds.

Note that these observations are limited to strong natural law theories because a strong natural law theory says that there is a decision procedure for *every* hard case. Perhaps the same objections can be made against more modest natural law theories. For example, one may hold a view of natural human rights that converts *some* ostensibly hard cases into easy ones. An instance would be an expansive view of natural property rights that converts all difficult tax and antitrust questions into clear violations of a personal right to noninterference with property. Such a view will always be controversial and may seem to rest on an arbitrary account of natural rights. But insofar as it is only a partial conversion of hard cases to easy ones, it creates hard questions elsewhere, e.g., at the perimeter of expanded property rights. It follows that such a view is imaginable and explicable, whereas a strong natural law theory, which claims to decide all questions, is inconceivable.

If we turn to theories that say that there may be mechanical ways of applying *positive* law, we find different but equally decisive difficulties. Here there is no problem about the source of the rules or about their legitimacy. A constitution, for example, both exists and is the source of legitimacy for other rules. But the strong theory of decision-making, in its positivist form, says more than this. It requires that the existing rules anticipate a specific resolution of all possible legal conflicts. Hart points out that this presupposes an untenable picture of human affairs, since human affairs continually involve new constellations of conflict, new demands, and new situations that no man-made set of rules could possibly anticipate.[18] Laws inevitably have what Hart calls "open texture." Is it tenable that the framers of the American Constitution could have anticipated unambiguous answers to the concrete civil rights issues of the 1870s or the 1960s, to the problems of economic distribution and control in the 1930s, to questions about the best allocation of diminishing natural resources or about individual rights in situations made possible by medical innovations like the artificial extension of life?

Note that a defender of the strong theory may defend his view in two ways, both difficult to sustain. He may say that a resolution of a hard case follows from the *letter* of the Constitution or that it follows from the framers' *intentions*.[19] The first position collapses once one concedes the obvious fact that the letter of the Constitution is controversial and indefinite in its application. The fall-back position, appeal to the framers' intentions, suffers from various difficulties. The intentions are not explicitly laid down as rules but are to be gleaned from records of debates, secondary writings, and incidental remarks. Of course, legislative intent must play a significant role in the judicial interpretation of legislation, and much has been written about its role. But it cannot play the role that the strong theory would have it play; it cannot determine an uncontroversial application of legislation in every hard case.

Two further points. First, there are obviously versions

[18] Hart, *Concept,* Chapter VII, Section 1.

[19] See, for example, the discussion of this point in Charles A. Beard, "Judicial Review and 'the Intent of the Framers,'" *Political Science Quarterly,* 27, 1 (1912).

of the strong position that admit that decisions cannot be deduced from the Constitution but that also say that decisions *can* be deduced from the Constitution supplemented by legislation. The same arguments can be replayed against this version of the theory. Second, since I am only considering strong theories at this point, I have said relatively little about the complex role of the intentions of framers or legislators in decision-making. It would be a foolish theory which would say that legislative intent ought generally to be ignored; it is impossible to read a piece of legislation and make sense of it without *some* reference to the intentions it would be thought to realize. On the other hand, there are sound arguments that say that legislators cannot ever anticipate all situations that the future may offer up, and therefore cannot have intentions with regard to unforeseen dilemmas. Thus, although I have considered some roles that legislative intent cannot play in judicial decision, I have not had much to say about the roles it can play. In pages 117–120 of this chapter we will look at the role of the history of a legal system as a resource in making decisions.

I shall now consider a different family of theories about decision-making. We have seen that it makes sense to conclude that no strong theory of decision-making is tenable. This is so whether the theory assigns a deciding role to natural law or positive law. It *seems* to follow that the law is underdetermined until judges decide, and therefore that law is "what judges say it is." This conclusion seemed compelling to a group of American legal philosophers in the early part of this century who have been called legal realists.[20] They saw

[20] In *Jurisprudence* (St. Paul, 1973), George Christie takes note of the following features of legal realism: distrust of the judicial technique of seeming to deduce legal conclusions from so-called rules of law, belief in the instrumental nature of law, and preference for behavioral explanation of legal phenomena. See Christie, pp. 642–644. Among the most influential legal realists were Oliver Wendell Holmes, Jr., Joseph C. Hutcheson, Jr., Jerome Frank, and Karl Llewellyn.

as part of their job the demystification of law and said that appeals to a strong and clear decision procedure invested the law and judges with omniscience and objectivity that they didn't and couldn't have.[21] In part they were simply acting as good historians, noting that the same Constitution had been used at the end of the nineteenth and the beginning of the twentieth century to encourage business expansion at the *expense* of regulation that would have protected individuals from exploitation, and used later in the twentieth century to protect employees, consumers, and others against the very same impositions by business interests. They noticed that incompatible political and economic commitments could and would be expressed in interpretations of the same Constitution and the same laws and that clear and unambiguous holdings could be overturned. They pointed out the apparent capriciousness of some judicial decisions that announced doctrines with no clear basis in political reasons *or* in the Constitution. The realists were not only historians; taking note of rapidly changing conditions—social, economic, technological; national and international— they endorsed a theory of decision and a view of the Constitution that could be flexible enough to meet unforeseeable needs and incorporate the policies of new generations of judges. They were not, of course, endorsing caprice. They were, however, describing the fact, the opportunities, *and* the abuse of an openness inherent in decision-making. The absence of a mechanical procedure of application was seen as part of the wisdom of the Constitution and not as a defect.

Legal realism has decision-making by judges as its main concern. Whereas a strong natural law theorist sees the judge as a mere transmitter of law, the realist sees the judge as the creator of law and therefore of

[21] See, for example, Oliver Wendell Holmes, Jr., "The Path of the Law," *Harvard Law Review,* **10,** 457 (1897), and Jerome Frank, *Law and the Modern Mind* (New York, 1930).

primary interest. Law is not simply what legislatures make because it is in the power of judges (*de facto* if not *de jure*) to emasculate legislation in practice.

Within this general framework, there are conspicuous differences among legal realists. Some are psychological determinists. They study and stress the psychological and nonrational bases of decisions and argue that a sufficient explanation can be given in this way. Although not a consistent determinist, Jerome Frank suggests that decisions are best understood by attending to the psychology of judging and of judges. We need to look not at the reasons given within decisions but the psychological causes, often uncovering irrational and unconscious motives. In this view, law is determined by objectively irrelevant conditions.[22]

Other realists see judges as lobbyists for special interests who disguise their bias with the rhetoric of objective decision-making.[23] Still a third kind of realist stresses that judges are lobbyists not for special interests or constituencies but for particular points of view about goals and values. In this view, judicial decision-making is properly an arena in which competing commitments are at war. This third version alone of the three takes seriously what judges *say* as a measure of their "real" reasons.[24]

Common to all forms of realism is the notion that judges, far from carrying out a decision procedure, are constrained minimally. To know how law is made, one must examine the actual process by which cases pass through the hands of judges and judges stamp decisions with their idiosyncratic characters or beliefs.

We have now looked at two very different kinds of theories about decision-making. In one view the judge is a mere conduit for law; in the other the judge has

---

[22] Frank, op. cit., Chapter 12.

[23] See Frank, *Courts on Trial* (Atheneum, 1949), *passim*.

[24] Compare Holmes, op. cit.

wide discretion, if not license. Although both address themselves to decision-making, it is not at all clear that they address the same questions about decision-making. This point is often obscured by the assumption that there is only one question, "What is the nature of judicial decison-making?" We already considered in pages 53–59 of this chapter some of the different kinds of questions embedded within this issue.

Consider one example of such unclarity. The positivist may be understood as responding to realism when he points out the secondary rules of law. Even if judges work out differing political and moral commitments competitively in the judicial arena, they do not have license to do just as they wish because there are formal bounds on what they may do. Certain ways of proceeding are impermissible; the secondary rules (on Hart's formulation) are a minimal threshold for judging properly, if not necessarily for judging well. Accordingly, law is not just whatever the judges say it is. Law is what judges say it is when and only when they are following the rules and procedures that tell them what to do. These rules may be entirely formal; they may tell them when to hear cases, how to report their decisions, and so forth. Or they may be partly substantive and may tell them what kinds of factors to weigh and what kinds to disregard.

Is this comparison of realism and positivism correct? The answer is by no means obvious. We need to consider two arguments that stand in opposition. According to the first argument the comparison is incorrect because the realist and positivist are asking different questions and engaged in different tasks. According to the second argument, they *can* be compared because the two so-called questions or tasks cannot really be separated.

The first argument is that the realist gives himself the task of *describing* what judges actually do; he investigates, for example, whether judges *in fact* are bound by particular secondary rules—and other constraints—or whether the claim that they do so is part of the mythology of law. He is a kind of sociologist of law. He is to be contrasted with philosphers of law who ask questions about the implicit standards that law and judging ought to follow. Part of the job of the philosopher is to find standards for what is permissible and for what is desirable in judging; the positivist has things to say about what is permissible. The fact that judges may often do what is impermissible, that they are hypocrites or are affected by psychological compulsions, is irrelevant to the project of sketching the standard of permissibility. A judge cannot *justify* his decision by saying he feels aggressive toward tall women or that he owns stock in defendant's company. The philosopher unlike the sociologist of law (for example, the realist) is concerned with questions of justification and not questions of description.

Unfortunately, this clear argument is not decisive, because *both* philosophers of law (positivists, among others) and sociologists of law can be said to describe what goes on in legal systems and both claim to be presenting "facts." The philosopher's "facts" are about the expectations, demands, and critical standards that persons bring to bear in examining judicial decisions. They are the same standards that judges are expected to use and to which, at the very least, they will pay lip service. These facts about standards of justification are not derived from an actual or hypothetical opinion poll; perhaps most persons and most judges could not produce their standards, if asked. The philosopher's claim is rather in the form of a hypothesis; in John Rawls's perspicuous phrase, it is the hypothesis that persons would uncover these standards in "reflective equilibrium"[25] if asked to sort out over time their

[25] Rawls, *Theory,* pp. 48–51.

responses to relevant situations for judgment. This means simply that a repeated process of setting forth a theory of standards of justice, checking that theory against intuitions about hypothetical cases, modifying the theory to fit the new intuitions, checking the revised theory against new intuitions, and so forth, will finally yield the theory of justice that Rawls himself offers.

The sociologist is working against the backdrop of a practice that involves the use of these standards. He describes their use and abuse. To understand his work, we see it not as a neutral description of behavior but as a description of (judicial) behavior that complies or fails to comply with justified expectations and standards. Thus, as a working premise we must assume that, however the standards are abused, compliance is possible. We must reject the assurance of universal hypocrisy or of universal overdetermination of decision by "unconscious" factors. We must, at our peril if it be otherwise, assume that judges in fact are actuated to some extent by the justifications they give.

Let's step back and see where our argument stands. We are questioning the statement that a sociologist of law (or legal realist) *describes* what judges do whereas a philosopher of law talks about what would *justify* what judges do. This distinction is easy to make and hard to accept. The reason is that philosophers *describe* standards implicit in judging and that sociologists of law describe what judges do, with critical standards implicitly in the background. If this is so, the distinction threatens to vanish. That is, it vanishes unless the sociologist or realist can argue that critical standards for judging *are* irrelevant because they have *no* role at all in decision-making. To say this is to take a deterministic view of the following kind. It is to claim that psychological drives and motives are all that ever affect decision-making.

In Chapter 4, I shall consider the implications and merits of deterministic claims. At this point, I shall argue that we have to reject them *or* stop short in our investigation of judicial decision. My argument is that to consider judicial decision we have to believe that persons are *capable* of making decisions. In other words, we have to believe in the *possibility* of moral agency. What does this mean? To believe that persons are capable of moral agency is to believe two very general things about human nature. The first is that persons are capable of making rational and conscious decisions; the second is that persons are capable of deciding to act and of proceeding to act for disinterested reasons, for goals other than personal gain. These notions obviously invite extended discussion, but we can briefly describe their relevance. Any discussion of decision-making within a practice or institution—whether we are talking about the decision of umpires, judges, or persons in ordinary moral situations—must involve assumptions about the *capacity* of persons to make impersonal decisions and to do so on the basis of the merits of the case. In other words, there is this choice: If one holds a deterministic psychological theory that denies this capacity, then one is committed to saying that all talk about permissible and desirable ways of deciding, and about the justification of decisions, is talk about a pretense and an illusion. If, on the other hand, one assumes the existence of the capacity, one sets a ground on which such talk becomes intelligible and appropriate. In affirming the capacity, one is not at all denying that unconscious factors often have a part in decisions or that persons often act for self-interest. But one *is* denying that unconscious determinants *fully* explain all decisions and that persons *always* by nature act in self-interest.

Postponing further discussion of this to Chapter 4, let's examine why it is relevant in assessing the claims of those realists who *deny* that judges can ever be disinterested and rational decision-makers. This would be to deny the *possibility* of judging cases by objective standards laid down by others and by the merits of the case at issue. It would follow that the conceptual issues that philosophers investigate and that are accepted in common sense rest on delusions about human nature.[26]

The special kind of realist who is a psychological determinist is not just doing empirical sociology and psychology. At the point at which he throws out ordinary assumptions about the possibility of being impartial and responsible, he is making a conceptual commitment (an assumption about human nature) that will bias the results. Faced with an *apparent* instance of disinterested decision-making, he will find in it a concealed goal of self-gain. No *possible* evidence can refute his assumption. It is important, therefore, to be alert to the fine distinction in practice between an empirical investigation and a methodological assumption. It is one thing to show that many decisions are self-interested; it is something else entirely to say that they are invariably self-interested because they cannot be otherwise.

In the rest of this chapter we will not pursue the preoccupations of realists. We will not investigate empirically whether judges comply with standards for making and justifying decisions or whether it is *possible* for them to do so. We will look at the prior (philosophical) questions of what those standards are and how they may be uncovered. Once the idea of a decision procedure that decides all questions mechanically is aban-

---

[26] I shall assume that this kind of radical critique of human nature can safely be rejected. In Chapter 4, I shall have more to say about a theory of human nature that allows us to make sense of responsibility, whether it is the responsibility of a judge, or of an ordinary individual making a moral choice, or of someone being held liable for a crime.

doned, some other account is needed of a judge's resources and of the resources that exist for criticizing the work of judges.

We saw above that conceptual investigation involves questions about what is permissible and about what is desirable in judging. If the argument in pages 51–59 is correct, the positivist[27] is responding to the question of what is permissible when he sets out a notion like that of secondary rules. This is only the beginning of an answer to the question of what counts as a justification for judicial decision, since it is hardly persuasive as a justification for a judge to say that he has done what is permissible, followed the outer bounds of decision-making. There is need to complete a theory of justification by asking what it would be desirable for a judge to do. This is the same question as what standards exist for criticizing judicial decision. If a judge has not done what would be desirable for him to do, he can be criticized.

Skeptical Doubts about Theories
of Decision-Making

In this section, I will consider two arguments that are attempts to show that the questions I have just raised are unanswerable and that we must stop short at this point. The first argument is that this is a doomed quest: there are no general standards for judging apart from whatever final but arbitrary standards have been set for the system. One system may commend the rigorous following of precedent, the strict application of past decisions to new cases. Another may commend deciding cases as unique opportunities for dispensing justice.

[27]I have Hart primarily in mind, but the same point (with a change of terms) can be made with regard to other positivists.

This response is based on a mistake about the level at which the question of standards will be addressed. We have seen that although two systems may have altogether different primary and secondary rules—one may have a constitution, the other not; one may proscribe religion, the other may enforce a state religion—we can in some respects discover features common to both. We can characterize the structure by virtue of which they are both legal systems. For example, Hart's definition and Raz's description are intended to be equally relevant to all legal systems. My hypothesis in what follows is that there are also general features of judicial justification. One way of uncovering these features is to confront the differences among the standards commended to judges in differing systems and to ask whether there are common goals (ends) to which these various standards can be means. If there is rigid respect for past decisions (a system of following precedent) in one system and ad hoc decisions in another, we can ask whether *both* are ways of addressing the function of combining stability and predictability of law with a consideration for the unique merits of the particular case. Such a reconciliation of values may take different forms, but the underlying goals may nonetheless be shared.

There are two obvious limitations to such a project. First, we may not succeed; there may be no goals that are the underpinnings of judging well in general rather than in particular systems. Perhaps reasonable persons—and reasonable judges—will differ about the implementation and character of even the most general goals in decision-making. The second limitation is that we may uncover standards of *legal* justification that are not necessarily standards of *judicial* justification. How could this be the case? We know, to begin with, that in any legal system decision-making responsibility is divided among lawmakers, judges and juries, enforcement officials like prosecutors and the police, and others. The limits and responsibilities of each role are set out in the secondary rules of the system. It may be that we would discover two things. First, that the system as a whole has certain distinctive purposes and goals, but, second, that the goals attached to the role of judges are so variable from system to system that nothing general can be said. In other words, we would be able to consider the justification in general for what the legal system as a whole brings about, but there would be no *general* way in which judges would be expected to make their decisions.

I shall assume that this is not so. I shall assume that the standards of judging are analyzable across different legal systems and that the concept of good judging is relatively independent of the nature of the legal system. The proof of this will be in the doing of it. If it turns out that we fail to devise a plausible account of judging, this caveat suggests a possible reason for such failure.[28]

---

[28] A lively debate about constitutional decision-making is related to the point just made. It is concerned with the claim that if we examine our own system or any other constitutional system of government, we will face the following irreducible distinction. Given a division of powers among the branches of government, it is the job of legislators to set rules in accord with policies and principles and it is the job of the judiciary to apply the rules *without* reassessing these policies and principles. In the absence of a decision procedure, that is, in the face of open texture of a constitution and legislation, judges must follow particular formal rules of decision, for example, the rule that ambiguous provisions be construed "strictly." To do otherwise is to encroach on the legislative prerogative by implementing substantive political, economic, or other policies. This objection could be raised for any system in which legislative and judicial functions are separated.

It is uncontroversial that judges are not legislators and that some justification can be given for distinguishing their functions. But it is not obvious that the difference as formulated above is either correct or feasible. First, let's clarify what may be intended by advocating "neutral" principles of decision. As used by many writers, "neutral" does not mean "formal" as opposed to "substantive." But what does "neutral" mean? Herbert Wechsler, in an important and controversial paper (see note 29) implies that a neutral principle of decision is one that has high generality and visibility and is not affected by the preferences of the decision-maker or limited to the constraints of the particular case or of a particular political or social circumstance. Wechsler is not commending formal principles

A different misgiving about the project is this. There are many kinds of judges, from judges in traffic courts who impose fines and other penalties for misdemeanors, to judges in family court who decide custody problems, to judges in Federal appeals courts. Philosophers of law tend to look mostly at decisions of the Supreme Court with the result that the evidence for their theories comes from difficult Federal appeals. Can a general analysis of decision-making by judges proceed in this way? It may seem, on the contrary, that an analysis of appeals decisions cannot be generalized. The work of the traffic court judge is essentially mechanical; the

---

that are neutral in content; to the contrary, he is urging that the principles of decision *be* substantive principles.

An example of a neutral principle that is often commended as a *formal* principle is ostensibly the principle of strict interpretation. The principle is often used ambiguously. Is it satisfied by (a) strict adherence to the text of the Constitution or to the intentions of those who adopted the text or by (b) decisions implementing a narrow view of the rights that individuals may legally vindicate against others? In many cases, these two interpretations of the principle will lead to opposite results. Taking strictly the notion that Congress shall make no law abridging freedom of speech may result in a broad rather than a narrow interpretation of that right of individuals.

We can use (a) and (b) to illustrate two obstacles to the formulation of formally neutral principles. In the first place, (b) is a so-called neutral principle that masks a substantive (or ideological) position. An ideological defense must be given for construing such rights narrowly. In the second place, a more general principle of narrow construction will need supplementation by substantive principles. Accordingly, a theory of strict construction may be implemented by decisions to the effect that the power of Congress to interfere with private industry are to be construed narrowly *or* it may be implemented by decisions to the effect that the freedom to engage in unregulated business activity (e.g., when there is participation by business in interstate commerce) is to be construed narrowly. In either case, the principle is empty until it is completed substantively.

There is a second way in which formally neutral principles fail, and this is illustrated by *both* (a) and (b). Here the problem is not with the ambiguity of standards but with the choice of standards in the first place. Why opt for a standard of strict rather than broad interpretation in the first place, whether the form adopted is (a) or (b)? Again, some substantive commitment will lurk behind this choice. A commitment to narrow construction will typically reflect a conviction that courts function badly— that they are inefficient, likely to abuse power, likely to judge wrongly.

work of the family court judge involves serious if not exclusive consideration of the welfare of the parties at issue. Both, it will be said, have little in common with the appeals judge.

A related objection draws a distinction between constitutional cases, cases in which the constitutionality of official actions or of legislation is in question, and all other kinds of cases involving criminal and civil claims. When legal theorists give primary attention to the deliberation and decisions of Federal appeals judges, they seem to assume that constitutional litigation is the model for all litigation. Can such an assumption be justified?

———————

A commitment to broad judicial intervention will typically be defended with a demonstration that individuals or other institutions will abuse power if unrestrained. We have already seen that the relationship between strict or narrow construction and minimal intervention is at best a contingent relationship; the identification of the two with each other rests on a confusion.

Our problem here is not to consider the merits of intervention and nonintervention but to notice that a *choice* between one or another principle of "neutral" interpretation reflects a substantive decision. Constitutions and other systems of rules do not ordinarily come equipped with an apparatus instructing judges in their application. To the extent that they do (to the extent that there are secondary rules of this kind) these principles in turn must be interpreted and applied by appeal to undetermined principles. Furthermore, we shall see that the theory of neutral decision-making (or of narrow decision-making) is not entailed by the need to distinguish between judging and legislating. The last sections of this chapter are an attempt to give an account that can be used for this purpose.

If the idea that there are neutral principles is inevitably tainted in this way, what can we make of the suggestion that judging differs from legislating because legislators do, and judges do not, implement substantive policies? One possible interpretation is that even if it is impossible to have strictly neutral principles, it is desirable for judges to *think* of themselves as following neutral principles. In other words it is desirable that they hide from themselves what they are in fact doing, choosing and interpreting "neutral" principles to fit substantive policies and commitments. This argument has a weakness typical of all arguments about benign myths. It assumes that judges ought not to face what they are really doing, that there is disutility in such self-awareness. Because this is a psychological argument, and therefore an empirical claim, it cannot be refuted by a conceptual investigation. Because it is implausible, however, the burden of proof must lie with those who would defend it.

These questions pose a powerful test for a theory of decision-making. It is obviously correct that American philosophers of law have primarily been interested in Federal appeals decisions. Interestingly, there is a body of literature on American constitutional decision-making and another body of literature on the nature of judicial decisions in general, but both are based largely on the same data.[29]

Whatever the origins of a theory may be, it is plausible that such theories *do* have general application. At all levels we can see equally well whether or not legal decisions are susceptible to mechanical determination. The objection that an unprecedented and unanticipated situation may arise is an objection that applies in every judicial domain. A recommendation that existing laws be applied so as to best realize justice has equal application in any court. There are three arguments for attending to decision-making at the Federal appeals level. First, it is plausible that the same kinds of standards apply at all levels but that they are most *visible* at the appeals level, where cases are usually hardest and where opinions are recorded and decisions are explained. Second, decision-making at the Federal appeals level in fact sets precedents for decisions at all levels. It is a model for decision-making in general. The third reason is probably the most important. It is that the test of an adequate theory of decision-making will be in its application to hard rather than easy cases, and hard cases are typically those that survive to the Federal appeals level.[30]

At the same time, a theory will fail if it explains hard

[29] In this respect, compare Wechsler, "Toward Neutral Principles of Constitutional Law," *Harvard Law Review,* 73, 1 (November 1959).

[30] The controversial character and importance of a case explicitly determine whether it is accepted and decided by the Supreme Court, which has discretion in such matters. The question of what standards of judgment to use is of course raised most acutely by the cases that the Supreme Court accepts.

cases but fails to explain easy ones. Thus, once we have a theory to examine, we must see whether it fits all forms of decision-making, including the apparently mechanical decisions of a traffic court and the apparently individualized welfare decisions of family court.

Legal Reasoning as Moral Reasoning

A moral decision, as I shall use the term, is any decision that can reasonably be expected to affect persons (or perhaps other sentient beings) in a beneficial or harmful way. To simplify, I shall limit my consideration to persons.[31] Judicial decisions are moral decisions because they affect persons by benefiting or harming them. A theory of judicial decision will therefore be a theory about moral decisions, but it will give special attention to the position and power of judges.

Let's see where we are in the course of our analysis. On the one hand, we saw that the elements of a decision procedure for judicial decision-making are not available. (In general, decision procedures are rarely available in human affairs because new circumstances presenting new dilemmas arise unpredictably.) On the other hand, judges do not have license nor do they have immunity from principled criticism. We identify *formal* parameters of what is permissible in decision-making when we identify the secondary rules that define what is permissible for judges to do, but this is only a beginning. Within the range of permissible procedures, there are sound and unsound ways of proceeding. Our job is to locate the very general standards, if they exist, that judges are expected to follow and that govern the criticism of judges. We saw that to find such standards

---

[31] There is a growing literature about moral rights of animals and of sentient beings generally. See, for example, Peter Singer, *Animal Liberation* (New York, 1975).

is to put forward a theory about justification, an analysis of what it is that counts as justification for a judicial decision and as a justification in criticism.

The situation I have just described in legal philosophy is really a general problem of moral philosophy. In the next few pages I shall try to explain the similarity by illustrating some of the following features of moral reasoning. Moral situations are of such complexity and unpredictability that the pursuit of a decision procedure seems fatally misguided. At the same time, it is not the case that "anything goes" in moral judgment. To be sure, there are no secondary rules, as there are for judges, that set forth *formal* designations and standards for moral judges; everyone is equally entitled, qualified, and expected to be a moral judge in relevant situations. Otherwise the conceptual problems about standards are quite the same as they are for legally empowered judges, as I shall now try to show.

It is easily seen why we are not likely to find a decision procedure for moral problems. Suppose, for example, that a president or legislator must decide whether to recommend using particular funds to improve a defensive missile system rather than to raise price supports for farmers. A moral debate about this decision will have to take into account many things: the likelihood that new defense systems will be needed for security, predictions about how such systems will be used, the economic circumstances of farmers, the effect on food prices, and many others. Such decisions are characteristically hard for two reasons. The first is that such factual determinations are complicated and uncertain. The second is that, even if such factual predictions could be made with certainty, different persons would weigh their moral importance (and strategic relevance, etc.) differently. This is not only true in a complex governmental decision. It is equally true in the case of a simple decision to break a promise to A (to meet A for lunch, for example) to help friend B (who needs help moving furniture). This is a fairly trivial case because the moral consequences of breaking or not breaking the promise are likely to be small, but even here the same difficulties are present. I cannot anticipate the results of my acts with certainty, and I am not likely to weigh the expected consequences of either action exactly as another person would. To suppose that there is a decision procedure for moral problems that *eliminates* these difficulties and to seek that procedure is to pursue a chimera.[32]

Notice that the difficulties are not relieved if one believes that morality consists in following rules that are strict and unqualified, rules like "Always tell the truth," "Never take the property of another without permission," "Keep your promises," and so forth. There is still the problem of what to do when the rules conflict. What if telling the truth *involves* breaking a promise? One may argue that there are other rules that specify which rules have priority over others. An example would be "Keep promises unless they involve lying because truth-telling has priority." But surely this is not very persuasive. There are some cases, easily imagined, in which a lie is justified because the adverse effects of breaking a promise would be very dire and other cases in which this is not so. It will now be suggested that this only shows that the rules need to be refined further. But counterexamples will always be available; the task of refinement can never be completed.

If it seems plausible that there cannot be a moral decision procedure that prevents real dilemmas from

---

[32] Kant, among others, claims that such a procedure exists, and that it generates clear solutions, at least with regard to promise-keeping. (See note 41.) In discussing objections to utilitarianism in pages 91–106 of this chapter I discuss the view that to take promise-keeping seriously as a moral commitment is to be committed to keep all promises. I criticize this view, and the criticisms are relevant to Kant's position.

arising, it is also plausible that not anything goes, that
not all *ostensible* moral opinions about situations are
intelligible *as* moral opinions or, if intelligible, are
capable of being seriously entertained. For example,
someone who said that in general it is morally good
to break promises or to maim philosophers would not
simply be understood as holding a permissible and
interestingly original moral view. Instead, such a person
would lead us to think either that he was misspeaking
(did not say what he meant or didn't understand how
to use the language) or that he could offer a special
ulterior justification, e.g., that promise-breaking tests
the mettle of the would-be promise, benefiting him by
making him self-reliant and tolerant of disappoint-
ment.[33] Such a reason may still be unpersuasive and we
may dismiss it, but it is intelligible while the bare
original claim is not. Similarly one who argues for the
moral merits of a policy that is said both to increase
the likelihood of war and to decrease the availability of
goods puts us on notice to expect a special reason why
such consequences are to be sought.

There are two ways in which a moral claim, a claim
that an act would be morally good or bad, can seem
unintelligible. The first, as we have just seen, is a claim
that endorses an act that is *prima facie* bad and does
so for no redeeming ulterior reason. The second is a
claim to which moral considerations simply seem
irrelevant. The claim that it is good, in itself, to clap
hands or make objects blue is a claim of this kind.
Again, the claim can be redeemed as a moral claim only
if a special kind of second-level justification is given,
for example, that clapping is healthful exercise or that
blue is an especially pleasing color.[34]

---

[33] A third possibility is simply to regard the speaker as crazy.

[34] This argument is elaborated and defended in my paper, "Goodness and
Benefit," *Journal of Value Inquiry*, IX, no. 1 (Spring 1975). See also
P. Foot, "Moral Beliefs," in Foot (ed.), *Theories of Ethics* (Oxford, 1967).

These very general remarks suggest some general conclusions about moral reasoning, because they lead us to ask what features of moral claims makes them understandable *as* moral claims. The examples suggest that there is *some* connection between the judgment that an act is morally good and the judgment that someone or other is benefited by it. What is peculiar about the claim that maiming or clapping hands is good is that there is no connection to benefit, and the criterion for a relevant explanation is that it establishes some connection of this kind. I am using "benefit" in the very general sense of "affecting someone in a positive way." The examples illustrate this point. The person affected positively may in some cases be the actor. It may be commended to me as morally good to cultivate my talents not because others will gain but because I will be better as a result.[35] Just as there is a connection between goodness and benefit, there is a parallel connection between the judgment that an act is morally bad and the judgment that someone is harmed by it. So far I have not tried to *examine* the connection beyond suggesting that it is a necessary minimal condition of sincerely calling an act "good" to think that someone is benefited by it.

I am not at all suggesting that there is a decision procedure for determining what things are benefits or for weighing benefits. I cannot expect that another person will agree with me on all my claims about what is beneficial or on my judgments about relative benefit, but I *can* expect that the reasons I give will tend to be understandable to him and vice versa. I can also expect that various particular and general differences in factual

---

[35] Note that not all consequences that are morally significant when A brings them about for B are also morally significant when A brings them about for himself or herself. It may be morally praiseworthy to feed a hungry child but not to have a meal when one is hungry oneself. Significantly moral self-regarding acts require a special account.

belief will often underlie and be available to explain our differences when they arise. I may believe, for example, that it is bad to discipline children by locking them in rooms; someone else may defend it on moral grounds. The difference between us may well turn to be a difference in our beliefs about the psychology of children. I may believe that such punishments create unresolved anger and mistrust between parents and children and are not effective in bringing about greater responsibility. A contrary belief about psychological facts will most likely lie beneath a contrary moral judgment.

We can also see why there is *rough* congruence in moral judgment.[36] Each person's notion of benefit has two components, some sense of the ways in which all persons are benefited in similar ways because they have similar needs, wants, and pleasures, and some awareness of the range of different personal ways in which persons are benefited—and of the reasons for these idiosyncracies. The fact that we successfully anticipate and understand the reasons that others give when benefit is discussed, whether we agree in our conclusions or not, is evidence that we have a shared sense of what benefit is.[37] To say that terms like benefit and harm (and

[36] What is the community of moral judges to which "our" refers? That community is certainly not defined by or limited to those who share a particular language. Rather, it is characterized by those who can recognize and understand moral situations and dilemmas, whether they appear in daily life, in Plato, Rousseau, Proust, Kierkegaard, Kawabata, or a contemporary mystery novel. The members of such a community will decide moral cases differently but will share criteria for the relevance of moral reasons and will grasp the sources of their disagreement. Obviously, this notion begs many questions about criteria of membership in such a community, about reciprocal understanding, and so on.

[37] This is not a special feature of the notions of harm and benefit but a feature of all notions, from such concrete ones as that of chair or food to such abstractions as happiness or liberty. I am here making a *logical* point: for terms to have common usage they must be understood in more-or-less the same way by users. Related arguments are to be found in Ludwig Wittgenstein, *Philosophical Investigations* (New York, 1953), *passim*.

goodness and badness) refer to a range of factually specifiable consequences for persons in general is to give a *naturalistic* account of them.[38] It is naturalistic because it says that certain substantive things or kinds of things are essentially good things to bring about and because it thus ties the moral notion of goodness to a particular factual content. By contrast, a nonnaturalistic account would explain the use of a term like goodness by a formal feature, for example, by saying it is the expression of a strong preference.

To summarize, I have suggested by example why there is not likely to be a decision procedure for moral reasoning and why, at the same time, there are some substantive standards for what counts in moral reasoning (*"not* anything goes"). This analysis depends on the link between goodness and benefit and on the *relative* determinateness of the notion of benefit. Although there is no objective measure for benefit, those who discuss benefit reach mutually understandable conclusions on the basis of shared criteria.

Before pursuing this argument further, I want to anticipate some responses and objections. (1) A possible response to my analysis is this: "If there is no decision procedure for moral reasoning, so much the worse for moral reasoning. Lacking a decision procedure, it is a defective form of reasoning." This response imposes a unreasonable Procrustean demand. There may be imagined advantages to a decision procedure for moral judgment just as there may be such advantages to knowing the future with certainty. (It takes little imagination to see there may be disadvantages as well.)

[38] The first step of a naturalistic account of our criteria for benefit would be to examine shared desiderata of survival. But an account of survival is only a minimal account of benefit. Note also that a naturalistic account of benefit would attend to differences among persons as well as similarities; A may naturally be benefited by *x* while B may naturally be benefited by *y*. These are facts that they may understand about themselves and about each other, facts that can then be a basis of moral action.

But the envisaged form of life is not *our* form of life nor is it a form of life that persons have ever had or can ever expect to have.

(2) A variation on the first response is that if no decision procedure exists moral and legal reasoning are not worth serious study. The investigation becomes a topographic survey of the terrain, an account of what persons happen to do when they make moral or legal judgments, and of whether they happen to agree or disagree. If we *could* generate a decision procedure, this would give a test for determining when judges (moral or legal) do their job badly or well. In the absence of one, we have no such test.

This objection rests on a misunderstanding. The misuse of the metaphor of topography shows this clearly. The "terrain" is not just surveyed and described. The moral and legal judgments made in particular cases are the philosopher's raw material not the end product.[39] The philosopher uncovers not only the judgments persons make but the *standards* that they use to arrive at judgments and to criticize the correctness of judgments.

This point was discussed earlier in this chapter. It is a general point about practices in which judgments can be made by using objective standards but in which there is, nonetheless, no method of deciding hard cases unequivocally. Just as there are standards for judging satisfactory moral decisions, there are standards for judging satisfactory cars, good cuisine, outstanding football playing, and good driving. None of these involve a decision procedure that yields the same judgment by all judges or in all contexts. There will be unresolved controversies about all these matters. None, on the other hand, involves license on the part of the judge to say anything he pleases on grounds chosen at random. It would not make sense to judge

[39] See the discussion of this point in Chapter 1, pages 5-10.

football by the standards of ballet. A different way of making my point is that it is wrong to say that judgments are *either* objective or subjective if *objective* means "made according to a decision procedure" and *subjective* means "made without recourse to publicly shared standards." Judgments that are involved in most activities are neither.

(3) Still another objection says that unless I can claim that there exists a decision procedure (that moral and legal judgments are objective) I can neither expect nor demand that others will share my views or my conclusions. This objection is in fact very similar to the second objection. What we have seen is that whereas I cannot expect others to reach all the same specific judgments that I reach, I inevitably expect them to have the same standards of judgment. I will, in particular, expect others to have the same criteria for what kinds of reasons are relevant, to weigh reasons in anticipatable ways, and to justify odd-sounding conclusions in anticipatable ways. This expectation is not coercive. It is not a "demand." Rather, it is a fact that *unless* they act in this way, they will not be participating in a shared activity ("practice") of judging. We will not be talking about the same activity.[40]

(4) A point to remember about legal and moral reasoning is that we expect decision-makers to act in a disinterested way. This means that in making a moral judgment, one must put aside one's own particular interest in the result and attend to benefits and harms for others.[41] As we saw above, when we talk about

[40] There is a sense in which certain odd-sounding claims about benefit, harm, and value may be intelligible as pathology. For example, the claim that clapping hands is harmful and dangerous and therefore morally bad may have to do with the particular significance that clapping has for the victim of a psychological disturbance. But this is not to understand the claim as a debatable moral claim made on the basis of criteria.

[41] To choose disinterestedly is to choose without any particular or *special* regard for oneself. This is not to say that effects on oneself must be dis-

moral reasoning and moral action we presuppose that individuals have the capacity to lay their own immediate interest to one side; a psychological theory that denies this will deny the possibility of moral judgment.[42] This matter is particularly clear in the judicial context. The fact that a decision may help or hinder a judge in personal or professional interests must be irrelevant to the decision. (This is a basic standard whether or not judges in fact lapse in this way.)

In this section I have tried to lay a foundation for a theory of judicial decisions by sketching the outlines of a theory about moral decisions. My assumption in doing so is that a judicial decision is a kind of moral decision, that what makes a hard case hard for a judge is that it presents a moral dilemma, or at least a difficult moral determination. If this is so, a judge can ignore the moral dimensions of his role only at his peril.

The moral theory we have considered has its beginnings in some simple observations. It says that there is a logical connection between moral judgments and factual judgments about benefit and harm, and that the moral goodness of an action or decision depends on its beneficial and harmful consequences. The theory formulated in this way will provoke contradictory responses. One is that it is obvious and empty. Who

---

counted completely rather than that they must be treated with the same regard as benefits to others. Kant makes the general point about disinterest in *Foundations of the Metaphysics of Morals* when he says that moral action involves treating others as ends in themselves and not as means toward achieving one's own interests. A form of the basic imperative of morality is to treat others in accord with a rule that one can will universally as a rule of behavior.

[42] Note the distinction between the deterministic view that individuals must always act in their own interest and the recommendation that individuals always act in their own interest even though they have the choice of not doing so. A variation of the latter view is the theory that it is always in one's interest to act morally and that one serves self-interest (at a second level) by being moral (on the first level).

would have thought that judges ought to function in any other way than to bring about benefit and prevent harm? It will be said that this is true and absurdly uninformative. A second, and very different, response is that the theory is radical and preposterous. Surely judges are constrained by standards other than the injunction to do good by maximizing benefit and minimizing harm! The result of judges following *this* rule would be chaos, the collapse of the institutions of law.

Clearly, the theory needs elaboration as an informative account of the standards that underlie moral and legal judgment. The theory is best explained by uncovering and answering various objections to it. I shall approach this job in three steps. First, I will fill out some of the details and applications of the theory by showing something of its pedigree. That is, I will show why it is a kind of utilitarian theory. But utilitarian theories are a family of different theories about moral reasoning and I shall show how our theory is related to other utilitarian theories. Second, I will look at some general objections that have been raised against utilitarianism and see which objections are relevant to our account. I will consider how those objections can be met. Third, and most importantly, I shall discuss the application of a utilitarian theory of moral reasoning to judicial decision-making.

Utilitarianism: Criticisms and Corrections

The motive behind nineteenth-century utilitarian theories is altogether different from our own motive. Jeremy Bentham, the "inventor" of utilitarianism, tried to devise a decision procedure for moral judgment, an intellectual strategy that would generate uniform objective solutions for moral problems and reduce all factors in a moral question to a common measure.[43] The present theory makes no such claims. It is not a mechanism for reforming the practice of moral reasoning; it is intended instead as a reminder and a perspicuous rendering of the standards that already inhere in the practice of moral reasoning as it is generally carried on. The notion of benefit is a notion we already have and employ. Let me explain these matters by raising particular points of difference.

In classical Benthamite utilitarianism, the goal of morality is to maximize pleasure and minimize pain.[44] Pleasure and pain are taken to be the common denominators of all morally relevant experiences. For other utilitarians influenced by Bentham maximizing happiness ("the greatest happiness for the greatest number"[45]) is the goal. It was quickly pointed out that there were difficulties in the Benthamite strategy because (a) pleasure, pain, and happiness are not measurable and (b) there are other moral goals besides pleasure, happiness, and the avoidance of pain. For example, it is easy to see that the pain of serious injury exceeds the pain of an inconvenient change of plans; an act that has the consequence of causing serious injury is therefore, for moral reasons, to be seriously avoided. But the question, how *much* worse is a serious injury, is an unanswerable question if it is a demand for a numerical answer. Much of Bentham's strategy seemed to presuppose that these factors can be quantified. The second objection can be illustrated by the moral value assigned to courage or self-sacrifice. Actions of this kind may benefit others and have altruistic motives, but they may do so by adding to the sum of dignity and self-

---

[43] Jeremy Bentham, *Principles of Morals and Legislation* (Oxford, 1948, originally published 1789).

[44] Bentham, op. cit., Chapters III–V.

[45] John Stuart Mill, *Utilitarianism,* various editions.

respect in the world rather than to pleasure and happiness.[46]

Objections of these kinds are irrelevant to a theory based on benefit and harm. The theory does not claim to give a decision procedure and acknowledges that benefit and harm are not measurable. What degree of agreement may exist in moral judgment is a function of the way (independent of theory) persons experience benefit and harm and not a function of mathematical reforms in judgment generated by the theory. The theory meets criticism (b) by demonstrating that the notion of benefit encompasses the moral goals that happiness, pleasure, and the avoidance of pain leave out. For example, by teaching someone self-discipline we may be benefiting him or her and therefore performing a moral act whether or not there is a net increase in pleasure or happiness.[47]

Modern critics of utilitarianism offer a criticism that is a variation of one just considered. Such critics as Richard Brandt[48] and John Rawls[49] argue that utilitarians advocate maximizing social welfare and that this leaves aside other important moral goals. Brandt offers the example of an aged parent who is artificially kept alive at great expense and with a heavy emotional toll on the family. Brandt argues that the utilitarian would

[46] See Richard Brandt, *Ethical Theory* (Englewood Cliffs, 1959), Chapter 15, for an account of these criticisms.

[47] Two points. This argument can only be carried out piecemeal. As each particular moral goal is considered, it can be argued that that goal is compatible with a theory of benefit and not with a theory of pleasure. The possibility of a counterexample (a moral goal which is not beneficial) cannot be ruled out but the burden rests with those who would disprove the theory. Second, note that it is always possible to save the theory that happiness is the sole moral goal by *redefining* happiness to coincide with the sum of moral goals.

[48] See Richard Brandt, "Toward a Credible Utilitarianism," *Morality and the Language of Conduct,* edited by Hector-Neri Castañeda and George Nakhnikian (Detroit, 1963), p. 109.

[49] John Rawls, "Two Concepts of Rules," *Philosophical Review,* **LXIV,** 1 (1955).

find no social welfare—and therefore no value—in keeping the parent alive. Rawls argues, to the same effect, that a utilitarian would be committed to breaking promises whenever some social welfare was to be attained by doing so.[50]

Such criticisms are not relevant to the theory of benefit and harm. Note first that the situations described or suggested by Brandt and Rawls in the examples are potentially very difficult. No adequate theory can generate easy answers and any adequate analysis will have to attend, more than Brandt and Rawls do, to the details of the particular situation. Where the prospect of survival, or of recovery of consciousness, or of diminution of acute pain is slight in the case of the aged parent, the dilemma will be hard. Analogously, there are cases in which promise-breaking is justified even though, in the absence of other considerations, there is likely to be harm to the promisee who has relied on the promise. For the utilitarian, promise-breaking will be justified only to the extent that the benefit to be derived through the breach overrides this harm. Thus, the first mistake that Brandt and Rawls make is in supposing that the answers to such dilemmas are obvious (that one preserves life at all cost, that one keeps all promises) and that the utilitarian answer *obviously* is the opposite of the correct answer.

The criticisms involve a second mistake that is more general and more important. They presuppose that all utilitarian theories (a) say that the moral worth of an act is determined by its consequences for welfare *and* (b) assign a specific weight to the relevant consequences. But the theory of benefit and harm explicitly does (a) and not (b). The significance or weight given to each factor in any moral situation is informed by our intuitions and by the usages that exist independently of the

---

[50] Rawls, op. cit., p. 17.

theory. Thus, in Brandt's case of the aged parent, the theory alone tells nothing about whether the benefit to the parent (and to relatives) of extended survival does or does not outweigh the suffering, expense, and so on. All it tells us is that when we *do* make a moral judgment, we must attend as carefully and distinterestedly as possible to considerations of benefit and harm, for what else is relevant? It is certainly possible and indeed likely that survival for one day may outweigh in benefit a great deal of suffering and long-term financial hardship; the utilitarian whose theory is based on benefit and harm would not necessarily say otherwise.

Having answered one set of criticisms, we must consider the objection that utilitarianism is an inadequate theory of moral reasoning in need of completion. In this view it is a vague or weak theory that instructs us to look for benefit and harm but that seems to allow almost *anything* to count as benefit and harm. Critics insist that it needs to be supplemented or replaced by a theory of rules (Rawls) or a theory of rights (Dworkin) that would identify particular kinds of moral consequences that would have priority over others. An example would be a set of moral rules that said that the benefits of liberty always have priority over material benefits.

I shall look in detail at theories of this kind but a general response is that my theory is only as elastic (or nonspecific) as the notion of benefit and that the elasticity of the notion must not be exaggerated. The philosopher's job doesn't end with uncovering the utilitarian principle, the relation of goodness and benefit. It also involves doing what J. L. Austin calls "linguistic phenomenology"[51] on the notions of benefit and harm to determine what sorts of things count as

---

[51] J. L. Austin, *Philosophical Papers* (Oxford, 1961), p. 130. G. E. M. Anscombe makes a similar point in "Modern Moral Philosophy," *Philosophy*, 33, 1-2 (1958).

benefit and how much divergence exists and can exist among those who use the notion. Those who find utilitarianism an inadequate theory seem to assume that this enterprise will yield little.

One form of this criticism is that unless we can say more about benefit we will have to give up making inter-personal comparisons. Unless there is an objective mea-sure of moral worth, formulated in rules of justice or a theory of rights, we must concede that what benefits a person is only what he *thinks* benefits him. Once we concede this we are no longer able to make moral judgments that are anything more than judgments about preference satisfaction. Accordingly, Ronald Dworkin claims that utilitarian theories collapse into theories that determine moral goals by looking at the preferences of those affected by the action.[52] This, Dworkin argues, entails fatal difficulties that will affect *any* theory in which preferences are a criterion for determination of goals, for example, a theory that says that happiness is to be maximized. Surely not all happiness is to count; what about the happiness of the sadist who enjoys the suffering of others? The same objection affects a theory of social welfare as long as social welfare is measured by preferences, by what persons claim (or think) they want. A society that has never experienced free speech or self-government may not include aspects of liberty in their notion of welfare. This should not mean that we *must* leave it out of account in considering their own welfare. This criticism clearly indicts a theory of benefit *if* the theory *defines* benefit by appeal to preferences.

Obviously, it is a sound observation that a theory that would define moral action in terms of maximizing personal preferences *is* a defective theory. But a theory that talks of maximizing benefit is not subject to this

[52] Dworkin, *Taking Rights Seriously,* pp. 233–238.

objection. The theory makes clear that, even if we assume that most persons most of the time are good judges of what is beneficial or harmful to them, being benefited and thinking that one is benefited are different matters. It is always possible to be mistaken. To the extent that these are different matters, to the extent that someone's sense that something will benefit him is only one factor among others in *my* judgment about what will benefit him, the sort of objection Dworkin presents is irrelevant. But, at the same time, a theory that meets the objection in this way invites the criticism that it is paternalistic. When a moral or judicial decision-maker claims that a decision will benefit A and B in spite of what A and B happen to think or prefer, the claim is frankly paternalistic. But is it to be rejected *because* it is paternalistic?[53] In responding, we need to distinguish two points. One is that there are perfectly ordinary situations in which an external observer may be expected to know what is going to benefit or harm a person better than that person. The observer may, for example, have special expertise. He may be a doctor, lawyer, engineer, or psychiatrist who knows that if the agent proceeds as he intends the consequences will, by the agent's own *eventual* admission, be disastrous. Even if it is conceded that paternalism has this limited justification, it will be said that paternalism is easily abused and the moral or legal judge will be tempted to override the preferences of the person affected even when he does *not* know better. Even more importantly the procedure seems to ignore the important benefits of being able to choose for oneself even when one chooses wrongly.

A brief answer is that *any* theory may be abused; it is no part of a theory to preempt its abuse. But, putting

---

[53] See Joel Feinberg, "Legal Paternalism," *Canadian Journal of Philosophy,* **1,** 105 (1971).

this aside, the objection is important because it is related to one of the most general and pervasive criticisms of utilitarianism, that no utilitarian theory can give proper attention to the moral importance of liberty and fairness. The rest of this section will be an examination of this criticism.

So far, we have clarified the theory that moral reasoning is in fact a matter of reasoning about benefit and harm by contrasting it with other kinds of utilitarian theories. Thus, it does not reduce moral considerations to a common denominator like pleasure, happiness, or social welfare. In doing so, it exempts itself from the criticism that it oversimplifies moral dilemmas or that it leaves out of account certain intuitions about the moral importance of life or of promises. It is, in other words, not a strongly revisionist theory that says that our ordinary moral intuitions are too complex and inconsistent; rather, it is a theory that takes up these intuitions and shows how they are to be reconciled. But if it is not an overly strong theory, it is also not a weak theory that says that the only justifiable goal identifiable in moral reasoning is the satisfaction of preferences (or want satisfaction). The theory, in invoking the notion of benefit, uses a notion that is strong enough to be used in criticism of preferences. It is a part of the theory that we are able to explain those situations of moral judgment in which we say that, wants and preferences notwithstanding, it is in the interest of persons to be compelled, for example, to go to school or to confront their responsibility, and so on.

Perhaps the most frequent and vigorous criticisms of utilitarianism say that no utilitarian can give a satisfactory account of the moral importance of liberty.[54]

---

[54] See, for example, Rawls, *Theory of Justice,* Sections 5, 6, and 30; and Dworkin, *Taking Rights Seriously,* Essays 4 and 12. Dworkin, unlike Rawls, opposes utilitarianism to theories of *rights* rather than to theories of liberty but the criticisms are similar.

revisionism - a movement in revolutionary Marxian socialism favoring an evolutionary rather than a revolutionary spirit.

Such critics emphasize that this point is particularly important when we are concerned with the morality of political or legal decisions. It is argued that an overriding interest in maximizing benefit and minimizing harm will inevitably lead (a) to decisions in which liberty is undercut for the sake of so-called benefit and therefore (b) to a situation in which persons are treated unfairly. The utilitarian is said to be led to these unfortunate results in two ways. First, his method of resolving cases will be to weigh liberty—when he considers it at all—as just one of several benefits that, as a class, are to be maximized. A failure to secure liberty may be offset by beneficial gains of other kinds. For example, a curtailment of free speech may be justified by an increase in material wealth overall. Second, the practice represented in this method will be to impose a judgment about maximal benefit on others; this will inevitably undercut the liberty to choose how one will live and even to choose to harm oneself. Thus, these critics say that a utilitarian approach undercuts liberty in two significant ways, by arrogating to the decision-maker unlimited decision-making power and by the particular decisions that he is likely to make. It follows that a theory that takes liberty seriously will have two features. It will place "jurisdictional" limits on decision-makers, limits that respect the inviolable liberties of individuals, and it will involve criteria for decision-making that will give special priority to liberty over and above consequences of benefit and harm.

The criticisms, as I have summarized them, are well represented by Ronald Dworkin's *Taking Rights Seriously* and John Rawls's *A Theory of Justice.*[55] Dworkin makes the first suggestion that in a correct theory of moral/judicial decision-making enjoying liberty is not just one kind of beneficial consequence among

[55] See note 54.

others. Rather the possession of rights by individuals is a kind of *veto* upon decision-making, one that individuals have implicitly and decision-makers must respect.[56] Liberty, if it is understood to be the enjoyment of matured and concrete rights,[57] constitutes an outer bound on permissible interventions in persons' lives. Dworkin argues that this notion of a boundary limiting what decision-makers can and cannot alter is one that utilitarians cannot take seriously.

The second suggestion is made by Rawls when he offers criteria for just decision-making. One criterion is that considerations of liberty be "prior in lexical ordering" to considerations of welfare.[58] This means that the goal of insuring for each participant in a practice (e.g., each member of a society subject to a legal system) the most extensive liberty that is compatible with a like liberty for all[59] cannot be overridden in the pursuit of any allocation of wealth in the form of "primary goods" (largely material wealth), however abundant and however equitable the distribution may be. The point of both Dworkin's and Rawls's arguments is that a theory founded on liberty (or rights)[60] as *opposed* to a utilitarian theory accurately gives the standards implicit in moral judgment, particularly moral judgments relating to public affairs.

This indictment raises several independent questions. Do the critics represent utilitarianism correctly? Do their own theories yield clear alternatives? I shall argue that the critics misrepresent utilitarianism as it can be construed along the lines of the theory of benefit and offer alternatives that are themselves unclear, alterna-

---

[56] Dworkin, *Taking Rights Seriously*, p. xi: "Individual rights are political trumps held by individuals."
[57] Ibid., pp. 90–95.
[58] Rawls, *Theory*, Sections 8 and 11.
[59] Ibid., p. 60.
[60] See note 54 on differences between Rawls and Dworkin.

tives that *may* in practice give the same results as the utilitarian theory. Consider the following points.

(1) One assumption that may be implicit in these criticisms is that liberty is not the *sort* of good that a utilitarian can take seriously. This means that utilitarians characteristically attend to tangible and material ends and prefer quantifiable ends; the paradigm is the accumulation of property. It is clear that this accusation misfires. The notions of benefit and harm are neutral with regard to the tangibility of ends. (Even classical utilitarians spoke of pleasure and happiness, and what is less tangible than pleasure?)

There is a more subtle form of the criticism. Liberty, unlike pleasure or happiness, is not so much a *goal* of action as an aspect or condition of acting and living.[61] When we speak of liberty, we are thinking of the needs of persons as actors, as persons who make choices and are aware of doing so. This abstract conception stands in contrast to the equally abstract conception of persons as passive collectors of goods. A moral theory that has a place for liberty must be based on an active rather than a passive conception of persons.

Let's see how a utilitarian might try to meet this criticism. Obviously, he needs a rich conception of benefit and harm. Benefits are not just goods received and harm is not just material injury or deprivation of goods. One is benefited whenever one is allowed or encouraged to act in a way that furthers self-esteem, self-improvement, the development of capacities, and the expressing and testing of one's thoughts. To be

---

[61] This is not to deny that securing liberty may be the goal of political activity. But it is a goal only in the sense that it is sought as a condition or aspect of other contemplated future activities.

The notion of liberty that I am using combines, I think, what Isaiah Berlin calls negative liberty ("freedom from . . .") and positive liberty ("freedom to . . ."). Liberty as a way of acting is positive liberty; liberty as a condition of acting is negative liberty. See Berlin, "Two Concepts of Liberty," in *Four Essays on Liberty* (Oxford, 1969).

provided with the conditions of living in this way is a benefit just as it is a benefit to have food, shelter, health care, and love.[62] I shall call benefits of the first kind "active benefits" and of the second kind "goods." It seems clear that active benefits can be secured only indirectly, by setting conditions for living well in these respects. The initiative for living well lies with the individual.[63] This does not mean, however, that these benefits are secured only by governmental self-abnegation, e.g., by noninterference with speech, assembly, and so on. They are also served by such affirmative interventions as compelling public education, providing mental health care, and preventing persons from interfering with the exercise of speech, and so on, by others.

The critics are correct that it is an important feature of an adequate moral theory that benefit and harm be generalized in this way. But there is no reason to think that a utilitarian theory of benefit and harm cannot meet this challenge.

(2) The criticism may be made in a different form, drawing attention not to the *kinds* of benefits the utilitarian can include within the theory but to the way in which he says we *compare* benefits in moral reasoning. Even when critics concede that utilitarians allow *some* weight to be given to the exercise of liberty, to self-esteem, and so forth, they claim that utilitarians will not be able to give them enough weight to generate a satisfactory account of their place in moral reasoning. This, we have seen, leads Rawls to say that there is a lexical ordering among principles of justice and that liberty has priority over wealth.

This objection is a variation of one we have already considered. The critic persists in attributing to the utilitarian a *particular* and a *counterintuitive* assignment

---

[62] I am not suggesting that the two kinds of benefits are commensurable. See discussion (text) following.

[63] Again, this is Berlin's notion of positive liberty. See note 61.

of weights to benefits. Once it is conceded that the theory *describes* moral reasoning as the weighing of benefits but *imposes* no weighing of its own, the objection disappears. It is entirely compatible with utilitarian theory that the moral decision-maker have a deep-seated commitment to "active benefits" and regard the recognition and fostering of the conditions of liberty as an extraordinarily important, and ordinarily supervening, way of conveying benefits. A moral/judicial decision that ignored or undervalued this range of considerations would be objectionable not because it was any more or less an instance of utilitarian reasoning but because it would rest on a mistaken conception of benefit.[64] If Rawls or Dworkin were to fault utilitarianism for failing to *guarantee* that liberty will be a supervening consideration, they would be looking for the guarantee in the wrong place. Recognition of the importance of liberty will be part of an adequate analysis of benefit.

There is one way in which the more general notion of benefit fits moral judgment better than a set of rules that give priority to liberty. There will always be special situations that are counterexamples to such rules, situations in which material needs are so urgent that a curtailment of liberty is morally justified. Governments justifiably declare curfews in emergencies, censor newspapers during war, and appropriate private resources to prevent starvation. A general rule of thumb that active benefits are supervening over goods is compatible with the recognition that in exceptional cases active benefits may justifiably be suspended to secure survival or mini-

[64] Of course the line between (a) inadmissible, mistaken conceptions of benefit and (b) the admissible range of views about benefit is itself a fuzzy line. Anti-Utopian novels by Orwell (*1984*) and Zamiatin (*We*) illustrate that there are easy examples of inadmissible conceptions. Furthermore, disputants who hold different admissible views will regard the other as mistaken and try to persuade the other of the mistake.

mal welfare. (This is analogous to the observation that promise-breaking will generally be harmful, given the expectation of reliance on the promise, but in special cases it will be justifiable.) In clearly exceptional cases it will *not* be justifiable on utilitarian grounds to adhere to the rule that gives priority to liberty, to allow starvation or to keep promises come what may.

Rawls admits that his principles will not apply to all situations, particularly not those in which scarcity or extraordinary dangers would make the exercise of liberty a matter of no significance.[65] He admits that a theory that offers rules of priority in assessing benefits tends to be caught between insisting that liberty is in principle a prior and overriding matter and admitting that there are situations in which goods are of primary importance.[66] Utilitarianism is not caught up by this seeming paradox because it rests only on the situationally variable notion of benefit. Exceptions to the liberty principle are just those cases in which the benefits to be gained by pruning liberty to prevent material harm are overriding.

(3) The problem with utilitarianism, according to a different criticism, is not that it ignores active benefits or that it undervalues them. Rather the problem is that a utilitarian decision-maker thinks of himself as *allocating* benefits, regardless of the nature of the benefits. To take liberty (or rights[67]) seriously is not to think of them as something dispensed but as a limitation on the kinds of allocations permitted to the decision-maker. They are a veto that individuals have over the range of possible decisions.

---

[65] Rawls, *Theory,* Section 38.

[66] I do not mean to suggest that Rawls himself is either unaware of this possible dilemma or caught in it. He argues that limitations on liberty in societies that are not well ordered are limitations that proceed from (and can be justified by appeal to) the principles of justice themselves. "Unfortunate circumstances and the unjust designs of some necessitate a much lesser liberty than that enjoyed in a well-ordered society." p. 243.

[67] See note 54.

It is hard to see what difference this criticism suggests *either* in the way decisions would be made *or* in the way decision-makers would generally think of their powers. By either the recommended theory *or* utilitarianism, the decision-maker intervenes to affect persons' lives. A decision to secure conditions for the exercise of freedom is still a situation that is affirmatively brought about. Respecting liberty or rights is not the same thing as refraining from a decision, not the same thing as refusing to make a decision. By refusing to act one may abet the infringement of liberty. If the practical point of the objection is not to recommend inaction by the decision-maker when rights are at stake, perhaps it is a point about the "demand" character of the decision. Perhaps it says that a decision to respect rights or secure liberty is incumbent on one in a way that the decision to maximize benefits is not. But this is a distinction without practical effect because the general principle of utilitarianism *already* makes it incumbent on the decision-maker to maximize benefit.

Lying behind the objection is a sound observation but one that has little to do with the merits of utilitarianism. The point is not about alternative standards or points of view for the decision-maker, because according to either theory he must not think of himself as inactive when rights are claimed and because (as I have argued) a utilitarian position may adequately capture his stance as a defender of liberty. Rather the point is about the attitude of the person affected by the decision. From this point of view, certain conditions that we call "rights" seem so clearly essential to the exercise of personality[68] that the decision-maker seems to have no choice but to convey these benefits. But this is an

---

[68] I am using the notion of personality in Max Weber's sense of the "understandable motivations of the single individual." See H. H. Gerth and C. Wright Mills, *From Max Weber: Essays in Sociology* (New York, 1958), p. 55. I do not intend to say that Weber subscribes to the view suggested about the relation of liberty and personality.

illusion. In hard or easy cases, the decision-maker chooses. The question is not whether he chooses but how.

(4) A final objection that may be raised is a psychological point and not a philosophical one. The point is that decision-makers who think of themselves as weighing benefits are likely to undervalue liberty and that decision-makers who think of liberty or rights as an absolute veto over conflicting benefits will in fact appropriately weigh so-called active benefits, and respect rights. It follows that the advocacy of a *self-conscious* utilitarian approach to decision will lead judges to make erroneous decisions

This is a strange argument. On one level, it is irrelevant because we are investigating the proper standards that ought to govern decision-making, the standards that are implicit in moral reasoning.[69] The notion that a decision-maker may abuse those standards is irrelevant. We are not investigating whether false standards *ought* to be promulgated among decision-makers as a prophylactic against abuse. In other words, we are concerned with the standards themselves and not with an examination of the benefits and harms of promulgating those standards.

Beyond this, the psychological assumption is unconvincing. It presumes that we know more about how moral decisions are made than we really know and that we know how judges would use or abuse particular standards. Furthermore, if the assumption about how judges apply standards were true, it would go far to undermine confidence in the use of *any* standards in moral judgment, whether they were the standards of the liberty-theorist or the utilitarian.

[69] See note 68. We are investigating the proper standards that "ought" to govern decision-making not from the particular point of view of the theorist's personal preferences but from the point of view of what is implicit in the practice of moral discourse.

Utilitarianism and Judicial Decisions

In discussing theories about liberty, we have noticed some special features of judicial decision-making. Unlike the decisions of an ordinary person in moral situations, a judge's decisions frequently affect liberties and ostensible rights. The objections of the liberty-theorist are raised most interestingly with regard to the decisions of public officials. In this section, I shall apply our general account of a utilitarian theory based on the notion of benefit to the decisions of judges.

There are constraints on judging that are not moral constraints; among these are formal and procedural rules. But all judicial decisions affect persons in beneficial or harmful ways. Decisions affect not only petitioners before a court, but also persons who will have to modify their behavior in accord with law as it is set in specific decisions, and even persons who merely have a general interest in the stability of government. In this sense, judicial decisions are necessarily moral decisions[70] and a general account of moral justification applies to them as well. And yet, as we have seen, judicial decisions have various kinds of beneficial and harmful effects that an ordinary person does not have to take into account. For example, a decision that may maximize benefit in a particular case may also (a) cause havoc in the legal system and (b) conflict with the formal criteria (Hart's secondary rules) of judicial decision-making. In addressing these distinctions, we must ask first how, in practice, a judge would go about making decisions in a utilitarian way.

First of all, note that in *every* moral decision some benefits and harms are direct and others are indirect. The direct effects are not necessarily weightier and the indirect effects may be overriding in determining

[70] See page 81.

the merits of an action. For example, White's decision
to break a promise to Brown in order to be available
to perform a service for Green has the direct consequences of harm to Brown (detrimental reliance, loss
of the object of the promise, and so on) and benefit
to Green. Indirect consequences are of several kinds.
Some are consequences for the immediate participants,
others are not. The decision may damage the friendship
between White and Brown, it may create a friendship
between White and Green, or it may undermine White's
trust among his friends generally. Other consequences
are more remote. The decision, if widely known, may
set a precedent for others in the community, may make
persons generally aware of and responsive to the plight
of persons like Green, and may weaken the institution
of promise-keeping. Obviously, the claim that a particular consequence will be significant depends on the
situation. (For example, it is often implausible that
breaking one's word will significantly damage the institution of making promises.) The general point is that
each of an indefinite array of consequences, near and
remote, are appropriately raised, evaluated, and perhaps
dismissed. The appropriate array of consequences to
consider is not defined as (a) the consequences of breaking promise x to Brown in order to, etc., but as (b) the
consequences of White's breaking promise x to Brown
in order to, etc. *Who* the decision-maker is and *how* he
is situated are often critically important in an assessment of consequences.

A judge in court is necessarily in a very different situation vis-à-vis the parties to a case than any other moral
decision-maker is to the prospective beneficiaries of the
moral judgment. A decision that Jones is liable in
damages to Kramer is altogether different from the
decision (and implementing action) of Robin Hood in
taking a sum equal to the assessed damages from Jones
and giving it to Kramer, even when the relationship

and mutual claims of Jones and Kramer are in both cases the same. As a utilitarian one is not concerned with the consequences attributable to the abstraction "deciding to transfer a sum as reimbursement for injury from Jones to Kramer" but with the consequences in the concrete situations of (a) Judge Tuck deciding in the state court of appeals that . . . and (b) Robin Hood deciding to steal from Jones, etc. The difference in context necessarily means that what I have called the indirect consequences will make a significant and possibly decisive difference between the two decisions. Judge Tuck, like Robin Hood, will consider as one element the history of relations between Jones and Kramer, the harm caused by Jones to Kramer, and the probable effect on Jones and Kramer of an award of damages. But there are other important elements present in Judge Tuck's considerations and *not* in Robin Hood's. Among them are the effect in general on business practices of parties relevantly like Jones and Kramer, the effect on other jurisdictions and other kinds of cases, the effect on public perception of judges and confidence in the law, and so on.

Judges, like others who administer and determine the law, affect society in ways that private moral decision-makers cannot. Even a highly visible, well-publicized private moral decision has no direct effect on other decisions in similar cases. It is not binding on other decision-makers however much it may have the force of example. Most legal systems, however, follow a system of precedent whereby a decision, once made, is binding on similar cases (the doctrine of *stare decisis*). Consistency is not an inherent feature of the collection of private moral decisions by various decision-makers or even by a single one. Consistency is, on the other hand, required of a legal system; rules enforced on behavior in a particular system or jurisdiction must be mutually consistent. This does not mean that there are no lapses in consistency but that it is incumbent on judges to reconcile decisions with the body of existing law.

I shall assume without argument that there is a general benefit in having a system of some public rules that are highly predictable and applied consistently, rather than a system of *ad hoc* decisions without discernible guidelines for future behavior. In other words, I assume it is desirable to have a system of laws over and above a system of private moral decision and action.[71] The consequence for the role of judges is that they must regularly attend to two kinds of beneficial/harmful consequences of any decision. The first kind involves both direct and indirect benefit and harm to those who have relied on existing law in its consistency and stability. Whenever a judge contemplates a decision that changes the law, he is likely to impinge upon and damage the interests of those who have relied on standing law. There are many general doctrines in the law that are designed to minimize this kind of dislocation. The *doctrine of precedent,* the doctrine that decisions should generally not be given *ex post facto* application (assuring that those affected by changes in law be in a position to be warned of the change), and the doctrine that a decision that represents a change be made on the narrowest available grounds are examples.[72] The generally beneficial consequences at stake when these doctrines are applied are reliance on settled law and consistency of treatment between parties to old and new cases.[73] The second group of beneficial and harm-

[71] Presumably an anarchist would disagree. Hobbesian arguments about the desirability of coerced order can be used to sustain the point.

[72] See discussion in Alexander Bickel, *The Least Dangerous Branch* (Indianapolis, 1962), and Richard Wasserstrom, *The Judicial Decision* (Stanford, 1961).

[73] Wasserstrom lists other purposes like certainty and efficiency, but I find it unconvincing that certainty is a separate virtue, distinct from reliance, or that efficiency is an independent virtue at all. In other words,

ful consequences are the effects of a decision on the parties to the case, direct and indirect benefits and harms to the petitioner and the defendant. In many cases, of course, a decision advances both groups of considerations at once; by adhering to settled law, a judge may benefit the parties to the case. In many hard cases, however, there is conflict; in these cases, considerations of justice to the parties to the case must be weighed against unsettling the law.[74]

The array of considerations of benefit and harm that a judge must consider is still more complicated than has been indicated. In every decision, a judge uses a rule of law to govern the case being considered and relevantly similar cases. Among the benefits and harms that are affected and must be weighed are not only (a) benefit and harm to parties at issue and (b) general considerations of predictability and reliance on settled law but also (c) benefit and harm to all subsequent parties likely to be affected directly or indirectly by the decision. Richard Wasserstrom, in his book *The Judicial Decision,*[75] gives the example of a foreclosure proceeding by a bank against an impoverished widow. From the perspective of Robin Hood, the widow's benefit seems to outweigh any possible benefit to the bank in allowing foreclosure. A judge, on the other hand, must consider the general effect of the practice that is being set up by the rule of the decision. The judge must anticipate, for example, that banks, knowing that enforcement of mortgage terms will be hampered in similar cases, will refuse to give such loans and

there may be some comfort in knowing where one stands vis-à-vis a stable but unjust law but no comfort at all in knowing it will be applied efficiently.

[74] I am using "doing justice to the parties" as a synonym for "maximizing benefit among the parties." Thus, I assume the arguments of previous sections have been accepted. The dilemma I am describing is the main subject of Wasserstrom's book.

[75] See note 29.

mortgages with the predictable consequence of great harm to the class of widows in similar straits.[76]

A judge will characteristically have to be more conservative than a private moral agent because considerations of kind (b) will count against decisions to change existing law and thereby disturb expectations built upon existing law. Considerations of kind (c) will in many cases, but not all, also have the effect of standing in the way of change. For example, the effect of refusing to enforce the terms of the mortgage in Wasserstrom's example is to damage future widows. A judge will do so reluctantly and will have to find countervailing benefits. On the other hand, in a case in which corporations limit their warranty coverage on products so that consumers cannot recover for defects, a change in the law that extends greater protection to consumers by outlawing such limitations may be justified in terms of the interests of parties to the case *and* of others similarly situated.[77]

Wasserstrom's discussion of judicial decision-making is also concerned with the complexity of a judge's moral decisions. I shall clarify the theory I have been offering by comparing it with Wasserstrom's perceptive analysis.[78] Wasserstrom identifies two unsatisfactory procedures for judicial decision. The first is based only on considerations of stability and reliance. He calls it the model of precedent; it gives priority to those considerations that I have labeled kind (b). The second model is based on considerations of fairness and justice to the parties to the immediate case (considerations of kind [a]); Wasserstrom calls it the equity model. Wasserstrom

---

[76] Wasserstrom, *Judicial Decision*, p. 108.

[77] See *Henningsen* v. *Bloomfield Motors, Inc.*, 32 N.J. 358 (1960), as discussed by Dworkin, p. 23ff.

[78] Wasserstrom's entire book is about the three models of judicial decision-making, the defects of the first two models, and the virtues of a "two-level" procedure.

concludes that a utilitarian committed to weighing benefits and harms in the *individual* decision will follow the second model. He argues that a modified two-level utilitarianism is needed to combine the virtues and avoid the defects of the two procedures: at the first level the judge consults established rules, and at the second he evaluates the rules in terms of their general effect in advancing the purposes of law.[79]

Wasserstrom's recommendation is ambiguous. Either he is proposing a procedure that will generate the same decisions as the straightforward utilitarianism advanced above because it will ultimately involve considerations of kinds (a), (b), and (c) or he means that *extra* deference should be paid to precedent considerations over and above whatever benefits are to be achieved by such deference. It is hard to see what can be said for the second position. By definition no benefit overall can be gained by instructing a judge to follow such an injunction except on the theory, rejected above, that judges be *instructed* to follow a different theory from the sound procedure they are *expected* to follow.[80] It is easy to see where Wasserstrom goes wrong. He assumes that a utilitarian who simply considers the consequences of decisions will be limited to considerations of kind (a), what he calls equity matters. But this is not so because the judge as utilitarian will be aware of his institutional role. As such, the judge will have to consider a range of benefits and harms beyond those that Wasserstrom calls equity matters, the range that includes (a), (b), and (c).

Therefore, a utilitarian theory of judging will not cause havoc because it will not involve *ad hoc* decisions made solely on the merits of claims by particular petitioners and effects on particular first parties. The mis-

[79] Wasserstrom, op. cit., Chapter 7.
[80] See pages 81–106.

understanding that it would do so seems to be the basis
of Wasserstrom's objection. A different criticism is suggested by Dworkin. It is that, whatever the merits of
utilitarianism as a moral theory may be, it is not the job
of judges to rectify misallocations of benefit and harm.
This is the job of legislators. The job of judges, unlike
that of legislators, is to apply laws and not determine
policy.[81]

This argument has both a crude and a sophisticated
form, although Dworkin offers only the latter. In its
crude form, it is the theory we were able to reject
above, namely that legislators have and should follow
a strict decision procedure whereby correct answers are
deduced from existing law. A sophisticated form is that
it is not the job of judges to formulate and implement
policies but only to safeguard principles of justice by
making secure the rights of individuals. The distinction
between policies and principles is at the heart of Dworkin's challenge to utilitarianism. A policy, for Dworkin,
is a standard that sets out as a goal "an improvement
in some economic, political or social feature of the
community."[82] A principle is a standard that sets forth
"a requirement of justice or fairness or some other dimension of morality."[83] "Principles are propositions
that describe rights; policies are propositions that
describe goals. . . . I shall distinguish rights from goals
by fixing on the distributional character of claims about
rights, and on the force of these claims, in political
argument, against competing claims of a different distributional character. . . . A goal [unlike a right] is a
nonindividuated political aim, that is, a state of affairs
whose specification does not in this way call for any
particular opportunity or resource or liberty for particular individuals."[84]

[81] Dworkin, *Taking Rights Seriously,* Chapter 4.
[82] Dworkin, *Taking Rights Seriously,* p. 22.
[83] Ibid., p. 22.
[84] Ibid., pp. 90–91.

I shall try to show that it is not obvious why this is offered as an alternative to utilitarianism[85] or that it would in practice generate different results. In the language of benefit and harm, we may say that the term *rights* identifies particular ways in which persons may be significantly harmed or benefited. These are harms and benefits so significant that (a) each person may think of them as conditions to which he is entitled and (b) only in exceptional cases can they outweigh other kinds of benefits and harms. Thus a utilitarian judge will give this class of benefits and harms a natural priority over others, not because they are expressed in principles rather than policies, but because they are weightier benefits.

One rebuttal to this argument is that the utilitarian practice does not *guarantee* that each person's rights will be protected whereas such a guarantee is an essential part of Dworkin's theory. Although this seems true on its face, there is a fatal difficulty. According to Dworkin, the only guaranteed rights are institutional ones (as opposed to background rights) and concrete ones (as opposed to abstract rights).[86] What does this mean? Among other things, it means that whether one has a right that *must* be respected depends on an assessment of the particular situation in which the right is claimed. But this is no more of an assurance than the utilitarian was willing and able to give in saying that rights are labels for benefits of supervening weight *prima facie* but that they must be assessed in particular contexts against competing benefits of comparable weight.

A different argument for Dworkin's position is that the contrast between rights and other benefits is so great and so clear that the utilitarian notion of a weighing or balancing is a misrepresentation of the process of decision. But the contrast is least clear where it is most

---

[85] Ibid., p. vii.
[86] Ibid., p. 93.

needed, in hard cases. To be sure, Dworkin is correct
that in ordinary cases decision-makers ought not to
prefer policy to principle because this seems to suggest
that they may disregard the rights of persons in effect-
ing social or economic goals. But this is not a distinctive
feature of the role of judges. It is the moral responsibility of all lawmakers. This is an abuse of proper decision-
making no less when it is done by legislation than when
it is done by a judge, and for the same reason. Thus,
both legislators and judges must attend to principles
as weightier considerations than policies, in general,
because principles tend to reflect more important benefits. But when we attend to hard cases, the distinction
between policies and principles does not seem more
helpful than the instruction to look for the most important benefits. In hard cases, how do we know what
is a principle and what a policy? That is, how do we
know what rights persons have? Is universal education
a policy or principle? Is it a right? Is providing minimal
subsistence a policy or principle? Do persons have a
right not to be allowed to starve? Indeed, it makes sense
to say that the protection of rights is itself a kind of
policy, a supervening policy for legislators *and* for
judges and, further, that cases are often ripe for judicial
decision when that supervening policy has not been
properly respected by legislators.

To summarize these criticisms, it is hard to see how
Dworkin's theory achieves clarification of issues that
the utilitarian theory fails to achieve. If the distinction
between policies and principles (between goals and
rights) is to have a special use, it must give us a special
identifying mark for rights so that we can recognize
when a right demands recognition, i.e., just when a
utilitarian weighing is said to be preempted by a right.
But what makes a case controversial and difficult is
precisely that we are unsure whether a benefit (usually
an "active benefit") is so important that it overrides

others and decides cases. Is, as we have said, the benefit
of being educated at public expense through the age of
seventeen a right supported by principle or a societal
goal described by a policy? Is there a right to be considered for law school admission without consideration
of one's race or is it simply one goal among others to
treat persons in this way?[87]

We must not leave Dworkin without noting and borrowing an important insight about judicial decision-
making.[88] A useful definition of a hard case is that it
is a case in which existing case law and statutes, the
existing system of judicial precedents, and other immediately relevant rules of decision tend to generate
or fit a result that offends the judge's intuitions about
benefit and harm. The legal system, as it comes down
to the judge, is not merely a system of rules or a system
of results, i.e., a system of particular allocations of
benefit. It is also a system of reasons. The development
of a legal system can be traced through the reasons that
judges have given for particular determinations, reasons
that embody many conceptions of human nature and
therefore of the ways persons are benefited and harmed.
The judge's matured decision must be informed by this
history. His own determination of benefit and harm
must be formed by consulting the justifications offered

[87]See Dworkin's discussion of this situation in *Taking Rights Seriously,*
Chapter 9. Dworkin repeatedly concedes that the distinction between
rights and goals is an elusive one: "It is hard to supply any definition
that does not beg the question. It seems natural to say, for example, that
freedom of speech is a right, not a goal, because citizens are entitled to
that freedom as a matter of political morality, and that increased muni-
tions manufacture is a goal, not a right, because it contributes to collective
welfare, but no particular manufacturer is entitled to a government contract. This does not improve our understanding, however, because the
concept of entitlement uses rather than explains the concept of a right."
p. 90.

[88]Dworkin, *Taking Rights Seriously,* pp. 105-130. The ensuing discussion in the text is my gloss upon Dworkin's story of a judicial Hercules,
and I am not at all certain he would accept my version of it.

by other judges in other relevant opinions. He cannot (as a matter of logic) accept all mutually inconsistent arguments and all points of view but must mold his own consistent standards around those standards that embody for him the values of the legal system itself. As Dworkin says, this task is described as an ideal and demands a judicial Hercules.[89]

It is important to stress the magnitude and nature of the task for two reasons. First, the utilitarian principle must not be taken to license the judge's disregard of the history of decisions and opinions in the legal system. It does quite the opposite, because that history is the repository of conceptions of benefit and harm in the face of which he forms his own conception. The second reason is that a redirection of the law by a decision in a hard case is one that must be justified by appeal to reasons that meet commonly shared criteria of relevance, criteria developed and illustrated in that history. There is all the difference there could be between saying correctly that these standards are incumbent on a judge and saying that he is narrowly bound by past decisions.

The Uses of a Theory of Decision

A theory that explains the nature of standards of decision-making, particularly moral standards, is not necessarily a theory that dissolves dilemmas. It may map the rough terrain that a decision-maker must cross but it does not make the terrain smooth. It would be fine, we might have thought, for philosophers of law to make hard cases easy—or at least easier, to tell us how to find right answers. Perhaps they can do so by telling us that judges exhaust relevant law at a certain point and have

[89] See note 88.

license beyond that point. Perhaps, on the other hand, they can tell us where to find natural law or how to identify those rights that decide cases and are formulated in principles of law.[90]

Utilitarianism not only disappoints all these expectations but explains why they must be disappointed. A decision about benefit and harm is a decision based on experience and ideally on wisdom, not a decision based on rules or license. A theory about decision cannot impart the stuff of experience, the appreciation of benefit and harm, any more than a philosophical theory about the nature of knowledge can impart knowledge about physics or history. Ironically (with some historical justification), utilitarianism is frequently criticized for having just such ambitions. We have seen that some forms of utilitarianism are vulnerable on those grounds.

The model of decision-making presented here allows us to give a synoptic account of well-known debates on constitutional theory. For example, such writers as Alexander Bickel and Felix Frankfurter, on the one hand, and so-called judicial activists,[91] on the other, debate whether it is generally wise for judges to intervene when controversial rights seem to be at issue and at the same time judicial vindication of such rights would significantly alter processes of social change. Bickel, following Frankfurter, commends what he calls the "passive virtues."[92] He means that courts should be reluctant to take upon themselves the responsibility for changing social practices in unforeseeable ways. He adds that the framers of the constitution anticipated such risks. One way of representing such debates (which

---

[90] Note, note 86, that Dworkin does not claim to make hard cases easy in this way.

[91] Compare, in this regard, Bickel's *Least Dangerous Branch* with any of several sympathetic discussions of the practices of the Warren Court or with the judicial opinions of William O. Douglas and Hugo Black.

[92] Bickel, op. cit.

the proponents may or may not find congenial) is to say that they are about what weight, as a general matter, is to be assigned to the benefits associated with the precedent model. They involve disagreement about the indirect or secondary effects of judicial activism.[93]

It is incorrect to think that self-conscious awareness of utilitarianism as a theory of decision is useless in such debates and, *a fortiori,* in resolving hard cases. Its use is elusive and indirect. It makes the discussant or judge aware of the standards of debate and the criteria of evidence. It makes explicit the process of fitting a decision within a general and publicly defensible theory of benefit and therefore of human nature.

---

[93] A secondary effect is a kind of indirect effect on the institutions of law and society.

3

Morality and Legislation

•

The "Enforcement of Morals"

Judicial decision-making has had the lion's share of attention from recent philosophers of law. Questions about the nature of law are often linked to questions about judging.[1] In Chapters 1 and 2, we considered whether law is essentially the decisions of judges, whether law preexists judicial decisions and constrains judges,[2] and whether morality is one of the constraints on the judge in making decisions. Judicial decision is only one of many points at which persons in legal roles

[1] See Chapter 1 and Chapter 2, pages 107–118.

[2] In a recent article, H. L. A. Hart diagnoses the special preoccupation of American jurisprudence with judges and the judicial role. He traces this to the functions that judges have in the American legal system and he compares the preoccupations of British and American jurisprudence in this respect. See H. L. A. Hart, "American Jurisprudence Through English Eyes," *Georgia Law Review,* 11, 969 (1977).

must take morality into account and may be criticized in moral terms. Legislators must consider the moral consequences of the laws they enact. Legislation loses its point unless it can be defended as benefiting persons or preventing harm. Also, ordinary individuals often have to face moral questions in deciding whether to obey laws. In all aspects—business, family life, recreation—personal lives are permeated by legal constraints, constraints that often raise moral dilemmas. In this chapter I shall consider morality in relation to legislation.

The phrase "the enforcement of morals"[3] has had great currency in debates that seem to consider whether law ought to be the enforcement of morals. I shall try to show that the question needs much clarification before we can begin to answer it. There is an easy way of seeing this.

Let's use the account of morality and moral reasoning that I defended in Chapter 2 as a version of utilitarianism. According to this account, the mark of a morally relevant reason is that it refers to benefit to persons. Now consider that every piece of legislation will in some way or other benefit or harm some persons. (It is hard to think of a significant counterexample.)[4] It is plausible that most reasons that may be offered in debates about legislation will be morally relevant in this sense: they will refer to ways in which the legislation would benefit or harm, and they will offer benefits as reasons for the legislation, and harm as reasons against it. It seems to follow that every piece of significant legisla-

[3] The phrase "the enforcement of morals" was chosen by Lord Devlin for an influential lecture and later for a book of essays on the relationship of morality and legislation. The debate he thus started is discussed in pages 136–163 of this chapter. The ambiguities of the phrase are very much present in Devlin's discussion.

[4] The benefit may come from the existence of a rule that creates order and regularity even though the exact contents of the law may be a matter of indifference. It is beneficial to have regularized driving patterns but driving on the left side of the street may be no more or less beneficial than driving on the right.

tion is an attempt to enforce morals since it is an attempt to benefit persons and to minimize harm.

Against this view, it will be said that laws achieve many sorts of social goals and are justifiable in many ways. We usually have economic, political, and cultural reasons for laws in addition to moral reasons. We have seen that Dworkin, for example, seems to have this in mind when he distinguishes between judges and legislators; judges are bound by moral principles and should decide cases by recognizing the institutional rights of persons, but legislators are doing their job properly when they implement policies of various kinds.[5] Even though Dworkin's account of the role of judges is controversial and even though others have argued that judges like legislators may generally take account of policies,[6] the main point about legislative reasoning seems to be unchallenged. Common sense echoes this view. There seem to be many reasons for tax reform, for legislation supporting cultural institutions, legislation defining the powers of the media or of monopolies, and so on, and only a small subset of these reasons and policies seems to be moral reasons and policies properly so-called.

A second argument against the claim that law is necessarily the enforcement of morals is one that I shall sketch briefly here and then discuss more fully. It is implied by Rawls throughout *A Theory of Justice* since Rawls's theory is clearly about public and not private decisions. This second argument uses assumptions

[5] Ronald Dworkin, *Taking Rights Seriously* (Cambridge, 1977), Chapter 4. See my criticisms of this distinction in Chapter 2, pages 114–117.

[6] See generally Kent Greenawalt, "Policy, Rights, and Judicial Decisions," *Georgia Law Review,* 11, 991 (1977). Greenawalt argues that the distinction between policies and principles cannot be sustained in the analysis of particular hard cases and that, therefore, judges may be said to implement policies. Dworkin admits that judges may properly decide on the basis of policies in those cases in which principles and rights cannot be said to be at issue.

about liberty and applies a distinction between private
and public actions. The argument is that moral standards are essentially standards for individual choice,
action, and criticism. It is the distinctive feature of
moral standards that persons can and should use them
as guides for action and as bases for evaluating the acts
of others. Relations among persons are private relations
by definition; the relation between persons and government is a public relation by definition. A government,
this argument continues, cannot make demands on the
same grounds that persons use in making moral demands
on each other. Some special justification must be found
for public encroachment on the natural liberty of
persons. This is not to say that moral criticism is irrelevant to the question of whether government should
intervene, but it is the beginning rather than the end of
the debate about whether there should be legal enforcement.[7] It is only part of the justification that would
need to be given.

I offer this argument as an initially plausible response
to the easy assumption that law must necessarily be the
enforcement of morals. It obviously needs expansion
and I shall look at it more closely.[8] For the moment,
however, we seem to have a dilemma. A simple common
sense argument that law is necessarily the enforcement
of morals is answered by two plausible arguments showing the opposite. But what seems like a dilemma is really
a muddle, because the phrase "the enforcement of
morals" has a different meaning in each of the three
arguments. Once we see this, we see also that each
argument contains a partial truth.

The first argument says that law is the enforcement
of morals, because law is a way of pursuing the maximi-
zation of benefit. We saw in Chapters 1 and 2 that the

[7]This statement is elliptical. The several questions that must enter into
a debate of this kind are the subjects of the various sections of this chapter.
[8]See pages 127–135.

premise of this argument is true, that it seems a sound if uninformative general characterization of the point of laws to say that their point is to benefit those subject to them.[9] It is also true that this kind of justification is a *moral* justification and, therefore, that a law justifiable in this way is a *morally* justifiable law. At the same time, we must avoid two equivocations. The first is equivocation between morality in the technical and rationalized sense of utilitarianism, in which it is tied to actual benefit and harm, and "morals" in the common sense in which it refers to popular attitudes of approval and disapproval of behavior. The two may not coincide at all. The second equivocation is between moral enforcement, i.e., the justification of the act of enforcing particular acts by weighing the benefits to be achieved by enforcement, and the enforcement of morality, i.e., the enforcement of those particular acts that *would* be justifiable in terms of their benefits *if* done freely and voluntarily, whether or not the enforcement of them as involuntary acts is justifiable. Clearly, our simple conclusion that the aim of legal systems is to produce benefits does not endorse the enforcement of "morals" or the enforcement of *whatever* would be justifiable if done voluntarily.[10]

The argument that says that not all reasons for legislation are moral reasons is an argument about "morals" and refers to popular attitudes toward private conduct, particularly sexual and social conduct. (This shows the derivation of "morals" from the Latin word *mores*,

---

[9] Note that this is a normative argument, an analysis of the general nature of any justification of a legal system. This may be true as a normative argument and be false as a description of legal systems, which may in fact be structured to deny benefits to those subject to the laws. According to the normative argument such systems are *pro tanto* not morally justifiable.

[10] Both of these points will be explained and examined; both are features of the controversy over Devlin's theory, which is discussed at length in pages 136–163.

which means "customs" or "conventional practices.")
In this sense, which is very different from the sense in
which we have been using the term *morality,* moral
reasons *are* different from political reasons, economic
reasons, and so on. In this view, whether a reason is a
moral reason depends on its subject matter. In the
technical utilitarian sense, economic and political
reasons that refer to economic benefits and social
benefits are themselves moral reasons.

I am not saying that so-called moral reasons based
on social custom and attitude must be a subclass of
moral reasons in the utilitarian sense, reasons citing
benefits. A social convention may be offered as a reason
for action whether or not it is claimed that the convention yields benefit. Thus, the argument that law ought
to enforce "moral" *conventions* is quite irrelevant to
the argument that law ought to maximize benefit.

Similarly, the second counterargument, which distinguishes private morality from public responsibility,
is also irrelevant to the claim that law ought to maximize benefit. There is a subtle but very important distinction between saying law ought to maximize benefit
and saying that it ought to enforce all behavior whereby
persons benefit others. Remember that the act of legally
(by public means) enforcing benefit-causing behavior is
certain to have its own costs, and these costs, which are
harmful consequences, may offset and even negate the
benefits.[11] The infringement of liberty is a general
notion that refers to the most important of these costs.

We have sorted out our muddle. What seemed to be
an argument and two counterarguments is now better
seen as three complementary claims. The first is that
laws need to be judged and justified by their contribution to overall benefit. The second is that such benefit
is not necessarily achieved by the enforcement by law

---

[11] The same points were made in Chapter 2 in comparing the consequences of a private moral act with the consequences of judicial enforcement of private morality. See pages 107–118.

of social customs and taboos. And the third is that such benefit is also not to be achieved by compelling persons to do any and all acts that can be urged in private moral reasoning. The claim that law is or is not the enforcement of morals often rests on confusion and equivocation among these three distinct propositions. But to straighten out this one source of confusion is only to introduce further matters, which are themselves controversial.

This section is a preview of several recurring themes in philosophical debates about the relation of law and morality and about the role of the legislator. Such debates often are about whether particular practices that are strongly held as social customs are the proper subject for legislation.[12] We have seen that it will always be important to ask the separable question whether such customs are also moral, whether they involve achieving benefit. Given a particular social practice, it is necessary to ask both (1) how the practice is related to benefit and harm, and (2) what part the answer to question (1) plays in deciding whether to make laws about the practice. The most controversial practices of this kind are those in which the nature and presence of harm and benefit are matters of urgent disagreement: unusual sexual practices, adultery, pornography, prostitution, abortion. Several of these practices are sometimes called "victimless crimes," and there are lively debates about whether they *are* victimless.

The Complex Relation of Morality and Law

Several points about the relation of morality to legislation form the background of any such discussion. I list and explain them here to set the stage for our main

---

[12] Devlin (pages 136–163) offers in *The Enforcement of Morals* (Oxford, 1965) an argument of this kind.

consideration and to explain the complexity of the relationship.

(1) We saw in Chapter 1 that Hart discusses what he calls the minimal moral content of legal systems.[13] Following Hobbes and Hume,[14] he points out that certain features of any known or foreseeable human society determine the content of legal systems. Some of these are features of human nature: vulnerability, limited altruism, limited strength of will, and approximate equality of natural strength. Others are features of the environment: resources are limited and there are predictable dangers to life and well-being. A minimal task for any legal system will be to provide stability and security in the face of such conditions.[15] Every system will control serious personal aggression, create a stable structure of centralized power, and arrange to distribute and exploit resources through regular channels. The *same* features of human nature explain some of our moral convictions, because they determine that persons are typically benefited in certain predictable ways and harmed in others. To the extent that these features are universal, the legal and moral response to them is also universal. In this way, morality and law coincide; legal systems inevitably have a predictable moral core.

Two clarifications. (a) Note that my point here is not that, as a formal matter, law and morality are both concerned with benefits and harms and therefore must coincide. The point is narrower. It is that *certain* identi-

---

[13] See H. L. A. Hart, *The Concept of Law* (Oxford, 1960), Chapter 9, Section 2.

[14] Hart acknowledges that this discussion is based on Thomas Hobbes, *Leviathan,* Chapters 14 and 15, and David Hume, *Treatise of Human Nature,* Book III, Part 2, Sections 2 and 4–7.

[15] This characterization is often used by social contract theorists who use the myth of persons coming together in a state of nature to set minimal standards for societal interaction. Compare Hobbes, *Leviathan;* Rousseau, *The Social Contract;* Rawls, *A Theory of Justice* (Harvard, 1971), Part 1.

fiable benefits and harms are so important and predictably universal that they occupy a central place in any moral or legal system. (b) The point being made is also *not* that a legal system will necessarily respond to these basic conditions in a way that can be approved from a moral standpoint. The legal system may respond by creating a very unjust system of distribution of resources or it may provide security at the cost of very severe curtailment of liberties. A minority may give itself privileges at the cost of enslavement of the majority. Again, the point is limited: even in a morally abhorrent society, some moral goals (some benefits) will necessarily be secured. Security and regularity will be achieved and, other things being equal, these are benefits.[16] But other things are often not equal. It may happen that a legal system, created in response to these minimal conditions, may bring about a degree of harm unheard of and unattainable in a state of nature or of anarchy.[17]

(2) There is one sense in which it seems that law can never be a vehicle of morality. To see this, we must distinguish moral consequences from moral action. By a moral consequence, I mean a situation in which benefit is achieved (or exercised)[18] or harm is minimized or prevented. By moral action, I mean acting to bring about a moral result with the *intention* of bringing about that result and for the *sake* of bringing about that result. Utilitarianism is a theory about moral conse-

[16] A comparable account of minimal moral characteristics of legal systems can be found in Lon Fuller, *The Morality of Law* (Yale, 1964).

[17] Whether one accepts this observation obviously depends on many assumptions. It depends on one's view of the state of nature; for Hobbes, any society that provides some security and regularity of affairs is morally preferable to the state of nature. It also depends on one's view of the kinds of abuses attainable under such legal systems as those of Nazi Germany and the Soviet Union in the 1930s and 1940s.

[18] It is odd to refer to a benefit being "exercised," but recall the discussion of benefits like freedom being conditions of action or opportunities for action, in Chapter 2, pages 101–102.

quences; it is a method for explaining why and how certain outcomes are morally to be favored over others. It prescribes a method of reasoning that can be used by those who intend to bring about morally desirable outcomes. But one may intend to bring about moral consequences without acting for the sake of those consequences. One may act morally for the sake of the good opinion of others and personal advancement. To be sure, someone who regularly seeks and achieves moral consequences is likely to be acting for the sake of these consequences and to be motivated by morality, but the question of motive is always a separable question.[19]

The point of this distinction is that legislators can compel persons to achieve certain moral consequences. They can even compel persons to act with the intention of achieving these consequences, with the intention of avoiding murder for example. They cannot, however, compel persons to intend these results *for the sake* of doing good rather than for some other motive, fear of punishment, for example. Law can achieve moral consequences by coercion, but it cannot compel persons to be motivated by the beneficial results themselves. In this sense, law cannot be the vehicle of morality.

There is, however, a less direct way in which law may be used to make persons be moral. Aristotle was the first and best exponent of the view that persons come to know what it is like to act for the sake of goodness *through* acting to achieve good results.[20] A society in which persons are compelled to act to benefit others is one in which the law may have educative value. Persons may begin by acting out of fear and end by acting because it has become second nature to have concern

[19] See Kant's discussion of this distinction in *Foundations of The Metaphysics of Morals.* See also C. D. Broad, "Conscience and Conscientious Action," reprinted in Judith Thomson and Gerald Dworkin (eds.), *Ethics* (New York, 1968).
[20] See Aristotle, *Nicomachean Ethics,* Book 2.

for others.[21] At the same time, we cannot dismiss the opposite view that legally enforced moral rules impede the natural moral development of persons, that the rule of law in moral matters prevents persons from learning to make their own choices and from engaging in moral debate. It substitutes an external for an internal judgment.[22]

We will not resolve this debate here. Both sides share, on the one hand, a positive view of the moral capacities of individuals and, on the other hand, a view that legal systems are able to affect moral development, albeit in different ways. It is possible to hold a view that denies one or both of these assumptions, a view that holds that most persons are not capable of acting for the sake of good results alone or that the requirements of law are insignificant influences in the moral development of persons. Perhaps all these positions contain partial truths. Perhaps some individuals more than others are capable of being morally autonomous, some more than others are affected adversely or positively by the law as a model of moral conduct, and some legal systems more than others affect moral conduct.[23]

(3) There are two kinds of moral actions with which the law, it seems, has no business. The first of these

[21] The acquisition of virtue through action and example is also discussed by Plato in *Meno.*

[22] The notion that man's natural impulses are corrupted by society in this way can be traced to Rousseau; compare *A Discourse on the Origin of Inequality* and *A Discourse on the Moral Effects of the Arts and Sciences.*

[23] The various opinions I have just discussed can, in some ways, be tested empirically. They also offer conceptual problems because they involve broad assumptions about human nature and psychological development. In a related context, Professor Elizabeth Anscombe wrote that progress toward solution of problems in moral philosophy—and even toward their clarification—must depend on prior investigations in philosophical psychology. This is relevant here because the relationship of legal constraint and moral motivation is underinvestigated and overburdened with theories. See G. E. M. Anscombe, "Modern Moral Philosophy," *Philosophy,* 33, 9 (1958).

is the class of supererogatory acts.[24] These are acts that
would convey benefit and/or prevent harm, but which
would at the same time be acts of unexpected or extraordinary generosity, charity, or courage. Ordinary
persons would not endanger or disadvantage themselves
in this way. There are two separable features of such
cases: the moral behavior involved is not ordinarily expected or demanded *and* the behavior involves considerable sacrifice. An act may be supererogatory if it
fills only the first condition: it is supererogatory to give
a match to a stranger vainly trying to light a pipe even
though the actor is very little put out. The second
condition usually accompanies the first and explains
why the behavior is not to be expected or demanded.[25]

Let's look more closely at this notion of moral expectations. In most situations, we can separate justified
expectations from excessive expectations even though
there will be many hard and controversial cases. As a
rule, I may expect a friend to keep appointments and
may expect a stranger to refrain from murdering me,
but I may not expect a stranger to give me money or
an acquaintance to sacrifice his or her life for me. If
we look at the class of justified expectations, we see
that there are two kinds, those that we have of strangers
and those that we have of persons with whom we share
some relationship. Another way of putting this is that
some justified moral claims simply depend on the fact
that we are all persons and others depend on the particular roles that persons have in relation to each other.
The claims and expectations one has of strangers are
largely negative; the general expectation is that others
will refrain from harming one's interests or oneself. The
claims and expectations we have of friends, colleagues,

---

[24] *Supererogatory* literally means "beyond what can be asked."

[25] The topic of supererogatory acts is discussed well by J. O. Urmson,
"Saints and Heroes," reprinted in A. I. Melden, *Essays in Moral Philosophy* (Seattle, 1958).

family, and so on, involve complex patterns of reciprocal benefit.

Within these categories of moral claims we must distinguish those categories that are suitable for reinforcement by law. We have already seen that law will ordinarily not be appropriate for enforcing supererogatory claims. The justification for this is both practical and theoretical. If a case involves great sacrifice, persons who would not volunteer to sacrifice may also choose to suffer the legal penalty for inaction *unless* the penalty is so severe as to outweigh the sacrifice. In practice therefore such laws would tend to be self-defeating. From a theoretical standpoint, it seems unfair to demand supererogatory action. (This observation would have to be backed by an account of fairness, which would lead us far into digression.) As we shall see later in this chapter, the notion that it would be unfair may reflect the sense that such coercion would be very costly in its effects on liberty and free choice. The enforcement of supererogatory acts would involve seemingly unjustifiable invasions. Note that we admire the person who willingly donates a kidney to save another person but that we would be justifiably fearful of a legal system that could require persons to donate organs while alive.

Another category of moral actions that is ordinarily not suitable for legal intervention are those *non*supererogatory claims arising from personal relations and roles. Let's compare these claims with those that are grounded simply in being a person *and* with those that are grounded in legal roles. A claim grounded in being a person is the claim that others, even strangers, refrain from murdering me. What is a claim grounded in a legal relation or role? Consider friendship as an example of a personal relationship and a contract or marriage (a particular kind of contractual relationship) as an example of a legal relationship. Laws are available to reinforce the moral commitments of parties to a contract, but they will not be available to reinforce the intricate bonds and expectations of friendship. There are practical reasons for this limitation. One important reason is that personal relationships that have not been transformed into legal relationships tend to be so complex and idiosyncratic in each instance—friendship is here a good example—that no attempt to formulate general rules for the practice can succeed.

I need to qualify and explain this last point. Although there are clear examples of legal relations and of purely personal relationships, there is a large middle ground. To what extent is the legal enforcement of moral expectations appropriate in marriage or in the family? To what extent within the relationship of teacher and student or doctor and patient? Legal intervention is clearly appropriate to some aspects of such relationships but not others. Indeed the character of such social institutions is continually redefined over time and change, whether this is desirable or not, tends toward greater intervention, toward a greater public role in setting and maintaining rules. A century ago the responsibilities of a doctor, lawyer, or teacher were set within particular relationships to patients, clients, and students and by the social expectations of the community; the imposition of objective standards for malpractice, for example, would have seemed an inappropriate idea. The situation is very different today.[26]

When is a moral relationship suitable for legal intervention? When is legal intervention justifiable? The most general answer is that it is justifiable when it does not have excessive costs, when it does not defeat the moral point of the relationship by undercutting mutual benefits or by harming the participants by infringing on important benefits that we conceive of as rights. In

---

[26] It is important not to underestimate the role of technological changes in altering relationships and particularly in depersonalizing them.

some kinds of relationships, as we have seen, the possibility of coercing the undertakings of the parties is incompatible with the adequate functioning of the relationship; in others this is not the case. Relationships of the first kind share certain features: success of the practice depends on the initiative and good will of the participants; appropriate actions must be defined as they proceed and as special circumstances arise; and the nature of appropriate behavior must be determined in terms of the talent, expertise, or sensitivity of the participants. This explains why the moral purpose of friendship would be likely to be defeated by legal enforcement, why only minimal requirements can be set or enforced for teachers, and why intervention in law or medicine is workable only where there are standard and invariant ways of performing.

Having looked in pages 121–127 at what is true and what is false in the assertion that law is the enforcement of morals, I have addressed three other aspects of the relation of law and morality. (1) Human nature and the human condition being what they are, there is necessarily an overlap in content between law and morality. Law almost inevitably seeks to provide those benefits that are essential to welfare and security. (2) An inevitable limitation on the use of law to bring about moral action is that law can bring about beneficial outcomes but not that persons be motivated by morality so that they act for the sake of benefit to others. (3) Another limitation is that law is not an appropriate tool to enforce supererogatory moral acts or moral acts within personal relationships based on skill or intimacy.[27] This examination of the relation of law and morality sets the stage for a detailed account of a debate that has preoccupied philosophers concerned with "the enforcement of morals."

---

[27]The theories of equal respect and of liberty that will be discussed (see pages 159–163) are attempts to explain and justify these limitations.

Lord Devlin, Mr. Mill, and Their Critics

An issue may take over the spotlight of attention by writers for various reasons. The reason may be its clarity or the opposite, its ambiguity. No doubt circumstances play a part; persons listen to that which they are ready to consider. In 1959, Sir Patrick Devlin, a prominent British judge, was invited to give the Maccabean Lecture in Jurisprudence to the British Academy. His title was "The Enforcement of Morals"; his topic was whether it is possible to offer a criterion for that realm of private morality that is none of the law's business. Devlin's treatment of this problem was provocative. Among contemporary writers in jurisprudence, Hart, Dworkin, Feinberg, and many others responded critically.

Three features of the debate account for its vigor. First, Devlin placed himself in an important position with regard to the history of political philosophy by using his lecture to challenge John Stuart Mill's position in *On Liberty*. Mill, as we shall see, tried to offer a criterion for limiting legal interventions; Devlin claims that Mill's arguments are fatally defective. Second, Devlin was responding to an inflammatory social controversy, the legalization of homosexuality and prostitution. Although these are the main applications he had in mind, his argument has implications for other controversies as well. And third, Devlin's argument can be seen as a contribution to the continuing debate between political liberals and conservatives.

The question whether there is a criterion that demarcates those areas of conduct that ought to be none of the law's business grows naturally out of the discussion of the enforcement of morals in pages 127–135. There I pointed out that some aspects of morals (customary social expectations and attitudes) fall outside a rationalized morality, where morality is the practice of maximizing benefit. One may take the position that a necessary (but not sufficient)[28] requirement for justifiable legal interventions is that they enforce rationalized morality and not just conventional attitudes. We will have to examine this claim with care in relation to Mill and Devlin. I also raised earlier the fallacy that any coerced acts would be benefit-conferring if they would confer benefit when done voluntarily by uncoerced persons; coercing has its own costs, harms that potentially offset the benefits. At the same time, some moral acts are properly the subject of coercion. A general criterion is needed for the threshold beyond which the costs of legal intervention are no longer morally justified. Such a criterion would also cast more light on why certain categories of moral acts are beyond this threshold, why the coercion of supererogatory acts or of the responsibilities of friends is not the appropriate concern of law. The debate that begins with Mill and continues through Devlin and his critics implicates all of these issues.

Mill's Legacy and the Wolfenden Report

Devlin's immediate purpose in his lecture and in the book that followed[29] was to challenge the arguments of the Wolfenden report, the report of a parliamentary committee created to recommend changes in laws that made prostitution and homosexuality criminal offenses. The report, issued in 1957, endorsed the decriminalization of homosexual acts between consenting adults. More generally it concluded that "there must be a realm of morality and immorality which is not the law's

---

[28] The requirement cannot be a sufficient condition for reasons that we have already considered (pp. 121-127): there will always be some benefit-conferring acts that lose their value as benefit-conferring when they are coerced. One reason is the cost (in harm) of coercion.

[29] See note 12.

business."[30] The committee followed Mill by distinguishing between crime and sin and saying that intervention by criminal law is justified only to prevent
intentional harm caused by one person to another. It
said further that this purpose is served by "preserv[ing]
public order and decency, [by protecting] the citizen
from what is offensive and injurious, [and by provid-
ing] sufficient safeguards against exploitation and
corruption of others, particularly those who are . . .
young, weak in body and mind, inexperienced."[31]
On the other hand, the job of law is not "to enforce
any particular pattern of behavior." In regard to both
consenting homosexuality and mutually consenting
acts of prostitution, the committee recommended decriminalization and rested its recommendation on "the
importance which society and the law ought to give to
private freedom of choice and action in matters of
private morality."[32]

The report borrows several strands of Mill's argument
in *On Liberty*. He says that it is indispensable, and
therefore a subject for criminal law enforcement, that
each individual in society "observe a certain line of
conduct toward the rest" that "consists, first, in not
injuring the interests of one another . . . [and] in each
person's bearing his share of the labors and sacrifices
incurred for defending the society or its members from
injury and molestation. . . . As soon as any part of a
person's conduct affects prejudicially the interests of
others, society has jurisdiction over it, and the question
whether the general welfare will or will not be pro-
moted by interfering with it becomes open to discussion. But there is no room for entertaining any such
question when a person's conduct affects the interests

---

[30] *Report of the Committee on Homosexual Offenses and Prostitution,*
paragraph 62.

[31] Ibid., paragraph 13.

[32] Ibid., paragraph 62.

of no persons besides himself, or need not affect them unless they like (all the persons concerned being of full age, and the ordinary amount of understanding)."[33] Three claims here that have sparked debate are (1) whether a line can be drawn between acts that affect others adversely and acts that do not; (2) assuming such a line can be drawn, whether that line is the appropriate line for sanctioning society's and the law's legitimate interventions;[34] and (3) whether Mill is correct in saying that society is not justified in intervening to protect persons "of full age and ordinary understanding" from acting in such a way that they are likely or certain to harm themselves. This last problem is the problem of justifying paternalistic legislation; I shall consider it separately in pages 163–174.

Mill offers a criterion of the sort we have been seeking. He distinguishes harm-causing acts ("prejudicial" to "interests") from other customary practices and says that only in regard to harm-causing acts is intervention defensible. He limits this class to harm-causing acts that are not done with the consent of the victim, and he does not permit intervention to compel beneficial acts that go beyond the prevention of such harm. He distinguishes not only between rationalized morality (harmful and beneficial acts) and other customary practices but also between the subclass of moral acts in which laws are to be used and the larger class in which they are not. In this larger class, the value of liberty (of being able to choose and of being able to act on one's preferences and decisions) outweighs the value of enforcing morality. The value of liberty is, in

[33] John Stuart Mill, *On Liberty,* Chapter 4.

[34] Mill sets different criteria for two very different kind of societal interventions, legal interventions on the one hand and informal social interventions (like isolation and condemnation) on the other. Informal interventions will be justifiable in many circumstances in which legal intervention is not justifiable.

turn, explicable in two ways. As we considered in Chapter 2,[35] it is a value in itself (a value incommensurable with others) to live freely. Mill, however, does not offer this justification for liberty but a somewhat different one. He argues that a society in which persons generally lead free lives is one in which the most productive and satisfactory ways of living are most likely to be uncovered and to serve as examples. According to this argument, liberty has instrumental value, value for society as a whole as well as for each individual.[36]

The Wolfenden report borrows all three features of Mill's argument. (1) It treats offense and injury as threshold conditions for intervention. (2) Imposition of such harm without consent of the victim, directly or through exploitation and corruption, is a further condition of intervention. And (3) individual freedom of choice and action is otherwise said to be an overriding value. (Note, however, a difference in language. The report uses the notions of "sin" and "private morality" to refer to those areas of conduct that I have called matters of customary social practice and attitude. Since the report distinguishes these kinds of conduct from conduct that is "injurious," I assume that "sin" and "private morality" do not refer to harm in a secular sense.)

In his own time, Mill's most serious critic was Fitzjames Stephen.[37] Foreshadowing Devlin's position, Stephen argued that Mill's criterion made no sesne and, even more importantly, that any attempt to set such a criterion for legal intervention made no sense. Rather, one must look always to the degree of harm or good involved in conduct. If the degree of harm to be avoided or of good to be achieved is significant, then

---

[35] See Chapter 2, pages 98–106.

[36] Mill, *On Liberty,* Chapters 2 and 3, respectively.

[37] James Fitzjames Stephen, *Liberty, Equality, Fraternity* (London, 1873). This is Stephen's major work in which his criticisms of Mill and his own version of utilitarianism appear.

compulsion to bring about such results may be considered. Moreover, compulsion is justified unless the cost of compulsion (the harm that is an inevitable part of coercion) outweighs the good to be achieved. "If . . . the object aimed at is good, if the compulsion employed is such as to attain it, and if the good obtained overbalances the inconvenience of the compulsion itself, I do not understand how, upon utilitarian principles, the compulsion can be bad."[38] Stephen saw this, as he indicates, as a straightforward application of utilitarianism.

This is not to say that Mill's approach is not a utilitarian one. Rather, Mill and Stephen represent contrasting uses of utilitarianism. For Mill, liberty is not merely a benefit that may be outweighed by other more considerable benefits in a case-by-case determination. The point that in modern society liberty is not to be weighed against public benefits can be made in the following way; it is possible to find evidence that this is what Mill intended to say.[39] Suppose one asked, from a utilitarian point of view, the question, "Who are properly the subjects of benefit and harm, the potential beneficiaries and victims?" An answer might be, "Free persons, persons capable of choosing and permitted to act on these choices." To the extent that tradeoffs between kinds of benefit and/or kinds of harm occur in a marketplace (metaphorically), the participants in the marketplace are free persons; they constitute the market. Their freedom, then, is not simply one of the goods that may be traded, one of the items about which they may negotiate in transactions. Rather, it is a condition that makes such transactions possible and significant. It is an aspect of life that is analytically on a

[38] Ibid., p. 50.

[39] The supervening importance of liberty in allowing "the highest and most harmonious development of [man's] powers to a complete and consistent whole" (Mill, quoting von Humboldt) is the major theme of Chapter 3 of *On Liberty*. This argument implies that liberty is incommensurable with other benefits or "goods."

different level from the market because it is a condition of the market. This is not to say that liberty can never be constrained or that limitations on it can never be justified. Nor is it to say that being free cannot appropriately be called beneficial. Nor, finally, is it to say that liberty has or ought to have this role in all societies or in all legal systems across history. But, in our system of justification and moral criticism, the constraining and limiting of liberty is not an activity that occurs in the marketplace, and the government is not just one of the participants in the market. A decision about liberty is a prior determination of what will or will not be *permitted* to be transacted in the marketplace. Still, that prior determination remains a decision made in a utilitarian way. It is a decision that, in the interest of maximizing overall benefit and of avoiding harm, certain matters may not be left to a piecemeal weighing of benefits and harms on a case-by-case basis.

Stephen, on the other hand, treats liberty as one kind of benefit that can be offset and undercut, case-by-case. And, in parallel fashion, he treats the costs of legal intervention as ordinary kinds of harm, not as involving special damage to liberty, special damage to the *ability* of persons to pursue harm and benefit. One way of showing the difference is to look at the claim that there is a special entitlement to dignity and self-respect that is antecedent to and a condition of being properly the recipient and conveyor of benefits and harms.[40] Mill would affirm this; Stephen would seem to deny it. They are both utilitarians, but of very different stripes.

Devlin's Arguments

Devlin challenges Mill in two ways. First, he rejects Mill's criterion for the point at which intervention is permitted. He builds on this argument by trying to show

---

[40] This argument is made clearly and at length in Chapter 7 of Dworkin, *Taking Rights Seriously.*

that there is no other point at which a clear limitation can be defended, no other point beyond which the behavior of persons is none of the law's business.

Devlin argues, to begin with, that Mill's conception of harm is arbitrary and narrow. Mill says that law may forbid behavior that damages not *any* interests of other persons but those interests that are embodied in rights.[41] In addition, society may through such informal sanctions as public opinion punish those who cause harm but do not violate rights.[42] The invasions of the rights of persons that may justify legal protection are individual and personal. They include not only unwarranted physical and financial injury, but also unwarranted restriction of liberty.[43]

Devlin argues that this is an incomplete theory of harm. He says that persons are affected in harmful and beneficial ways by all sorts of conditions in their society and all of this is potentially the law's business. The activities of others are part of the fabric of society. They affect public attitudes and thus shape the circumstances of life even for those who have no part or no interest in such practices. No actions are wholly private when all acts are made possible by and have an effect upon public attitudes. Specifically, Devlin says it is shortsighted to assume that only consenting participants are affected by homosexuality or prostitution. Toleration or nontoleration affects the quality of life for all.[44] This is particularly true when public media magnify trends and exaggerate changes; reporting such changes, they become the vehicles of change.

[41] In Chapter 4 of *On Liberty,* Mill says that society may enforce conduct that "consists, first, in not injuring the interests of one another; or rather certain interests, which either by express legal provision or by tacit understanding, ought to be considered as rights."

[42] The dicussion of informal sanctions in Chapter 4 of *On Liberty* follows the passage quoted in note 41.

[43] *On Liberty,* Chapter 4.

[44] See Devlin, *The Enforcement of Morals,* p. 16: "I do not think that one can talk sensibly of a public and private morality any more than one can of a public or private highway. . . ."

In this way Devlin challenges Mill with an expanded
conception of the individual's interests, whereby he
rejects the distinction between public morality and a
private domain that is not the public's business. All
practices are public because none are outside or independent of the fabric of society. It follows not only
that Mill's attempt to draw a line between harm that
demands public sanctions and acts that are of no public
concern must fail, but that any attempt to do so must
fail.

Once he has shown that, in principle, any practices
may have harmful consequences for persons who have
not elected to suffer such consequences, Devlin is ready
to face the question of how to measure these harmful
consequences. How is a legislator to know when the
harm is great enough to justify remedial legislation?
Devlin concedes that it is not enough to say that some
persons are offended by the practice or to say that the
practice would entail some detrimental changes in
society. But it would be too much, on the other hand,
to demand that the damage be demonstrable by an uncontroversial objective test before legislation be permitted. Devlin argues that if we can use legal institutions
to allow persons the opportunity to express and act
on their preferences, we may also use law to implement
such preferences when persons feel their society is
threatened by too much liberty, by license. For legislators to know when the damage caused by certain
practices is intolerably great, they must look not just
to the existence of adverse feeling but to the strength
and depth of such feeling in the community. They must
look for widespread "intolerance, indignation, and
disgust."[45]

It would be a mistake to say that, for Devlin, feelings
of indignation and disgust are themselves the harm that
justifies intervention. They are evidence of harm be-

[45] Ibid., pp. 15–17.

cause they are evidence of the extent to which persons would wish to resist such changes in society and to which they feel threatened. Devlin's contention is that as soon as legislators concede that the law may take account of relatively intangible harms, they are in the position of either imposing their own opinion about what intangible harms are to be resisted *or* of accepting a public consensus about this. And legislators have no warrant for imposing their own preferences in place of those of the members of society.

Devlin concludes that for the legislators to act otherwise would be illiberal and arbitrary in the guise of protecting liberty. Devlin admits that effects on liberty must always be weighed by the legislators and unnecessary incursions on liberty must be resisted.[46] But in cases where the popular sentiment is that collective well-being is profoundly threatened and where the future cannot be known, legislators have no basis for *denying* that liberty must yield. It must yield here if it yields anywhere. Only in cases where the popular will is weak or indefinite may legislators interpose their own sense of the importance of liberty. Here, as elsewhere, Devlin picks up a theme of Stephen's critique of Mill. We shall see in the next section how Devlin's many critics build upon the essential features of Mill's position.

Repairing Devlin's Theory

Devlin's theory was developed not only in his Maccabean lecture but also in a series of essays written in response to early criticisms of the lecture. There are therefore several versions of his theory.[47] I shall now examine the most important criticisms and see what

---

[46] Ibid., p. 16: "There must be toleration of the maximum individual freedom that is consistent with the integrity of society."

[47] Compare the first, fifth, and sixth essays in *The Enforcement of Morals.*

modifications or repairs would have to be made to meet them. In a few cases, there are repairs that Devlin himself began to make in later versions of the theory.

Several problems remain unresolved in Devlin's discussion of harm. One question is whether he distinguishes between change in the practices of society, or social evolution, and damage to society. In every society some persons have an interest in conserving received social practices and taboos. Such conservatism may have causes that have little to do with actual harm to society as a whole. (1) Some persons may in fact benefit from those practices. They may derive esteem, self-respect, or profit and therefore be damaged by change. For example, persons who are sexually inhibited because of personal reasons may feel secure and comfortable in a repressive puritanical society. Their resistance to change is not an indication that change will be harmful to society as a whole. (2) Persons may fear change for its own sake. Any period of change is a period of re-evaluation and therefore of risk. Many persons characteristically expect the worst. Thus, for understandable psychological reasons again, change is *seen* as a decline of standards, as a mark of decadence and license. Those who would in the end profit from such changes as well as those who would suffer may respond in this way. There is a natural resistance to the evolution of society. Persons reject the hard fact that practices that work well in one period can be made irrelevant or repressive by changes in science and technology, in cultural self-discovery, and in politics. At the same time, there is value (or benefit) in living in a society in which one feels at home, in which traditions and familiar practices give pleasure. Part of the importance of liberty is the opportunity to exercise it to maintain a comfortable environment. The dilemmas raised by resistance to change are therefore complex.

We must distinguish change from decline more clearly than Devlin distinguishes them. We cannot *assume* that any feared or unpopular change is a decline. If part of the legislator's job is to distinguish change from decline, public feeling is not likely to be a reliable measure. Note that Devlin insists that strong feelings and fears (indignation, intolerance, and disgust), rather than opinions and reasons, are what count in public sentiment. He says that the ordinary person must not be expected to give persuasive reasons to support strong feelings about the quality of life; if he fails to give reasons, his feelings may still be trusted.[48] But we have just seen that the strong feelings of persons who resist change or who insist on repressing certain kinds of behavior can often be explained in ways that have nothing to do with genuine harm to society.

We seem to be in a dilemma. If Devlin is correct that the legislator's own guesses about harm to the "fabric" of society are as unreliable as any others, and if *we* are correct in saying that popular sentiment must often be mistrusted, is there a third possibility? Ronald Dworkin's comments on this issue[49] point toward one solution. Dworkin recognizes that public attitudes toward social and sexual practices have many causes. One must take into account loss of familiar values, on the one hand, and prejudice and personal animosity and frustration, on the other.[50] The job of the legislator is to distinguish between "mere preferences" and reasoned opinions held on the basis of justifiable grounds. Strong

[48] Devlin, *The Enforcement of Morals,* p. 15: "English law has evolved and regularly uses a standard which does not depend on the counting of heads. It is that of the reasonable man. He is not to be confused with the rational man. He is not expected to reason about anything and his judgment may be largely a matter of feeling. It is the viewpoint of the man in the street."

[49] Dworkin, *Taking Rights Seriously,* Chapter 10. I have paraphrased Dworkin's argument loosely to match the terms I have used in explicating Devlin's views.

[50] It is important to avoid the opposite view from Devlin's, namely that the views of the man in the street are always to be discounted out of hand. Nonetheless, the manipulation of public feeling and sentiment for demagogic ends is a familiar experience in the twentieth century.

public sentiment is a *symptom* that there *may* be good reasons for legal intervention. Having identified those reasons that underlie public sentiment, the legislator must assess those reasons independently. Thus, he must be able to distinguish two kinds of responses to the decriminalization of homosexual behavior, "I abhor it" and "It is likely to have harmful consequences." He must consider whether the first response is a mere preference and must consider the second, *not* to determine how strongly the belief is held, but to see whether it is true. If supported by evidence, in this case that of experts in psychology and sociology, it will play a part in the legislator's decision.

What counts as a "mere preference" and what as a reason? Suppose the sincere reaction is not "I abhor it" but "It sickens me to know that homosexual behavior exists unpunished." Is this a kind of harm that a legislator ought to prevent? Compare this situation to a case in which persons are sickened through the failure of a public utility to provide pure drinking water. In the second case, we have no problem in saying that the legislator should pass laws to prevent this. There are three ways in which the case of homosexual behavior differs. First, persons can ordinarily avoid being distressed by the private behavior of others; they can take obvious steps to avoid exposure. This permits us to distinguish between legislation forbidding public nuisances from legislation affecting consensual private behavior. Second, if one pleads special susceptibility ("The mere awareness of the behavior distresses me"), one is admitting that we may not be able to provide relief, because general legal prohibitions can rarely be used to protect specially susceptible persons at the cost of a diminution of liberty.[51] We do not forbid

---

[51] Of course there are exceptions. When the effects of a product or activity on a small group with special susceptibility are very great and when the effects are not otherwise controllable, legal intervention may

the distribution of strawberries although some are violently allergic to them. The third and most important distinction concerns the activity to which objection is made. The involvement of persons as consumers of water is not incidental or avoidable. When the *essence* of an activity is to supply a commodity, the demand that the commodity be acceptable is *always* well grounded. To undertake a commercial activity is to assume an obligation and consumers acquire correlative rights.[52] In contrast, the claimed injury of a person who objects to homosexual private behavior is incidental. The participants have undertaken no obligation and are involved in no public transactions. The injury is not the direct and avoidable consequence of public undertaking that, if carried out properly, would have no such result.

Dworkin offers a way of seeing why one person's preferences with regard to the behavior of others ought to be discounted. He distinguishes between personal preferences, preferences with regard to one's own enjoyment of goods and opportunities, and external preferences, preferences with regard to the assignment of goods and opportunities to others.[53] He points out that a utilitarian assessment of benefits and harms that takes account of the satisfaction of external preferences will be corrupted "because the chances that anyone's preferences have to succeed will then depend, not only on the demand that the personal preferences of others make on scarce resources, but on the respect or affection they have for him or for his way of life."[54] In our

---

be appropriate. For example, doctors may be required to test patients for drug allergies before administering medications.

[52] This principle is not absolute; laws define the limits of the obligation and the correlative rights. The doctrine of *caveat emptor,* although less pervasive in law today than forty years ago, is still (perhaps inevitably) with us.

[53] See note 49.

[54] Dworkin, *Taking Rights Seriously,* p. 235.

example, a preference for pure water is a personal preference; the preference that homosexuals refrain from active sexual behavior is an external preference.

Let's summarize this criticism of Devlin. Expressions of "indignation, intolerance, and disgust" may be evidence of three very different kinds of reactions. They may express (1) personal preferences by asserting personal interests, (2) external preferences, or (3) reasons for moral disapproval by demonstrating how the interests of third parties are damaged. The legislator must take seriously expressions of kinds (1) and (3) and distinguish them from expressions of kind (2). Even with regard to (1) and (3), the legislator must not assume that intensity of feeling is an adequate measure of the extent to which the interest has weight in the making of laws. Rather, he must consider personal preferences of kind (1) as *prima facie* self-assessments of benefit and harm and third-person claims of kind (3) as *prima facie* evidence of altruistic moral convictions. He must be able to distinguish among (1) the claim of a member of a racial minority to equality of economic opportunity, (2) the claim of a racist that to provide equality of opportunity would affront him, and (3) the claim of a civil rights advocate that the protection of racial minorities from discrimination must weigh heavily in legislation. The objection to Devlin is that he claims that beyond a certain threshold the legislator must yield to intense public feeling; this allows external preferences to shape public policy.[55]

It can be argued that this analysis is sound but that it doesn't apply to Devlin because he is concerned entirely with personal preferences and not with external preferences. In this view, abhorrence and disgust express

[55] Ibid., p. 236. My argument in this paragraph is a reconstruction of Dworkin's argument. He is concerned to distinguish between my categories (1) and (2), personal and external preferences, and has little to say about my third category.

a sense of personal injury. They express the judgment that the toleration of certain practices is likely to bring about a change in society, a harmful change in the context in which one exercises one's freedom and has interests. If this is Devlin's claim, how is it to be answered?

One way is to admit that personal preferences are being expressed but to say that they do not give *sufficient* support to laws that forbid certain activities. The argument concedes that the objections are relevant but appeals to a common sense understanding of the weight of particular reasons, of particular harms and benefits. It is an attempt to show that the degree of suffering of the objectors is less than the degree of suffering of the victims of repressive legislation. It makes use of the argument that the significance of their suffering is diminished by the fact that they can avoid exposure to its primary cause and that they are otherwise the victims of a special susceptibility.

This response has two features. It concedes to Devlin that one cannot usually discount an opinion as an external preference when that external preference masks the claim that one is being injured oneself. It parts company with Devlin in stressing the relative independence of the legislator's judgment. One must weigh assertions of benefit and harm by one's own lights and with whatever resources and expertise one can muster. The response seems to reflect the common sense observation that legislative debate *does* seem to involve weighing such unmeasurable benefits and harms and that cases are not made easier by resort to principle.

Let's look at the implications of this "weighing" test. One consequence is that if the anguish of the objectors and the dislocation of social practices are great, the legislator *will* be justified in disallowing a liberalization. For example, if he believes that a valuable sense of community and shared traditions would be

jeopardized by decriminalizing homosexuality, he will
be justified in voting against such changes. He will also
be justified in limiting free expression whenever in
his considered view the social cost is too great.

This view is internally consistent and familiar in
political debate. It is also at odds with a set of opinions
about a legislator's obligations that have had much
influence in American political history, particularly in
recent opinions of the Supreme Court. In this view,
individual rights and individual liberty must not simply
be weighed against other benefits. They must be given
precedence and in some sense be treated as absolute.
For example, it is said that freedom of speech is worth
a great deal of inconvenience, worth even the near
certainty that it will have some long-term undesirable
consequences. This is not to say that there can be no
exceptions or that a commitment to free speech would
entail allowing persons to shout "Fire!" in a crowded
theater.[56] It is to say, however, that the simple weighing
test may not explain the precedence that ought to be
given to certain freedoms in face of predictable harm
and inconvenience.

I shall refer to the weighing test as the "repaired" Devlin theory. It is Devlin's theory modified to incorporate
the distinction between change and harm, the distinction between feelings and reasons, and the notion that
the legislators must weigh reasons put forward for or
against legislation independently and to their own best
ability. It retains the most important feature of Devlin's
argument, the claim that legislators must weigh the
claimed suffering of those who say they have a stake
in restricting certain liberties against the interests of
those who would exercise the liberties; as a result no

[56] This distinction merely describes the problem, of course. See, for
example, Thomas Emerson, *Toward a General Theory of the First Amendment* (New York, 1966), for a brief but authoritative account of the
judicial attempts to set and describe the limits of free speech.

criterion can be offered for those cases that are none of the law's business. Critics of this position argue that the legislator has a special moral role that this argument doesn't capture. It can be described in various roughly parallel ways: safeguarding those areas that are not the law's business, protecting the liberties of minorities from the will of majorities or the powerless from the will of the powerful, insuring equal opportunity and respect for the preferences of all persons. In the next section, I shall look at various ways of instructing the legislator how to do this job. Several such theories have recently been offered by Devlin's critics.

Note a pervasive contrast between Devlin's underlying assumptions about the relation of the individual to society on the one hand and the assumptions of his critics on the other. His critics, finding their inspiration in Mill, paint a picture of a legislator who deploys critical standards in opposition to popular will. He is to guard against excesses by using independent judgment, particularly in those cases in which benefits and harms are remote and speculative and in which the popular will may be shortsighted.[57] He is like a referee in a field of contending parties who has the responsibility to see that none gets the upper hand unfairly. Devlin's legislator, in contrast, has no special standards. In speculative or remote cases of harm to the fabric of society, he trusts his own judgment no more than that of anyone else and defers to popular sentiment as the only, and therefore the best, resource. It is assumed that popular opinion is formed from the same ingredients and with the same care as his own opinions are; in hard cases, he must take it as his guide.

Obviously Devlin's theory is best suited to a society in which the sentiments of persons can generally be

---

[57]Chapter 5 of *On Liberty* describes the applications of Mill's principles and implies that the legislator has a moderating role of this sort.

trusted to reflect considered judgments, in which there is a rough consensus about issues and goals, and in which there are few exploited extremes of power. It assumes that people are largely rational and good willed. In any other context, it can (in its "unrepaired" form) become a rationale for oppression and for a form of totalitarianism.[58] The theory benignly assumes that one can rely on human nature rather than on laws for basic safeguards. In contrast, a Millian theory is vigilant to the need for such safeguards; it will be put forward by and be suited to a pluralistic society in which persons cannot be counted on to be rational and beneficent.

Theories of Liberty and Equal Respect

There are two problems, a practical and a theoretical one, that a theory of legislation must seek to answer. Devlin's critics contend that his answer, even in the repaired theory, is an inadequate response to both problems. The practical problem, as we have already seen,[59] is that any legislative intervention in the affairs of persons has its special costs or harms. If a certain kind of activity, for example, the production of pornography, produces long- and short-term harm, the nonexistence of the activity may clearly be better than its existence. But the suppression of the activity by law may be *worse* than its existence. How can this be? The free choice not to sell pornography impinges on no values and has no costs. But the suppression of it impinges on liberty, on being able to choose one's activities. This may produce harm of three distinguishable kinds. It may harm the would-be pornographer by limiting opportunities for expression and commerce;

[58] See note 50.
[59] This is discussed and explained in pages 107–118.

it may harm persons at large by placing a check (which can be used capriciously) on the expression of ideas, on communication; and it may have a "chilling effect" on liberties in general by creating a climate of expectation that activities will be allowed or prohibited in unpredictable ways. To believe that suppressing may be worse than permitting the harmful activity it is not necessary to implicate all three kinds of harm in every situation. It is enough that at least one will have to be taken seriously in each situation.

So much for the practical problem. The theoretical problem, which would exist even if legal suppression had no costs, is to describe a way of thinking about law and morality that sorts out our intuitions about those cases in which suppression is not the law's business and those, like murder for profit, in which intervention is necessary and desirable.

Devlin's repaired theory, which endorses case-by-case weighing, is one answer to these problems. I shall now look at two alternative theories, both of which are inspired by H. L. A. Hart's distinction between positive and critical morality.[60] Hart says that this is the distinction between "the morality actually accepted and shared by a given social group" and "the general moral principles used in the criticism of actual social institutions including positive morality."[61] This distinction may mean several things. It *may* be read as the distinction between "morals," or prevailing social standards, and the critical or utilitarian standard that requires that they be measured in terms of standards of actual benefit and harm. We have adequately discussed this distinction.[62] We have seen that Devlin,

---

[60] See H. L. A. Hart, *Law, Liberty, and Morality* (Stanford, 1963), Chapter 1, pp. 17–24. Hart acknowledges that one source for the distinction is the writings of the nineteenth-century utilitarians.

[61] Hart, *Law, Liberty, and Morality*, p. 20.

[62] See pages 121–127 and pages 127–135 this chapter.

unrepaired, falls victim to confusion in this matter but that the repaired argument is not about undifferentiated strong feelings but about reasoned public sentiment about benefit and harm. A second interpretation of Hart's distinction is that it distinguishes reasoned public sentiment about benefit and harm, on the one hand, from the critical corrections imposed by the legislator on these assessments. The legislator reaches conclusions having weighed public sentiment as *prima facie* evidence of benefit and harm. We saw that Devlin's argument can be repaired to take account of this distinction as well.

The third and most important use (for our purposes) of the notion of critical morality is to distinguish between the *legislator's* assessment of benefit and harm and the question of what *limits* should be placed on the authority of the legislator to make decisions in terms of such a weighing. The notion that there may be such limits is put forward and explained by utilitarians as an aspect of "rule-utilitarianism."[63] This theory adapts utilitarianism to the situation of institutions in which decision-makers have delegated powers that are limited. The rule-utilitarian argues that such limits are justified, because there are cases in which greatest benefit is achieved not by letting a decision-maker determine maximal benefit in each case but by constraining him with certain rules. Neither the repaired nor the unrepaired Devlin argument is a theory that considers seriously what such limits would be and how they would be justified. The unrepaired theory says simply that in hard cases the legislator must defer to strong public sentiment; the repaired theory says that the legislator must weigh on the basis of a *prima facie* case set by public opinion about benefit and harm. The two

[63] See David Lyons, *The Forms and Limits of Utilitarianism* (Oxford, 1968).

theories that we shall now consider describe and justify such limits.

Rolf Sartorius's theory about the limits of legislative discretion sets out four plausible assumptions. It is an attempt to say when, as a general matter, liberty must not be infringed.[64] The first assumption is that in a broad range of controversial cases there is serious conflict between the value of liberty and the existence of behavior that is seen by some as seriously harmful, but there is broad disagreement about the nature of the harm and its severity. Examples are the free expression of sexual preferences, abortion, offensive and inflammatory speech, and prostitution. Second, Sartorius argues that the best *abstract* answer to the question when to intervene through law *is* given by the weighing test; the legislator is to determine when seriously harmful consequences outweigh the effects on liberty. But, third, he observes that when legislators make mistakes in trying to carry out the weighing test, they err by undervaluing liberty because it is an intangible and diffuse value.[65] Hindsight shows that legislators are bad prophets and they tend to repress unpopular practices, practices with which they have no personal empathy. Finally, Sartorius argues that there is no general standard for distinguishing those cases in which legislators are likely to be bad prophets from other cases. He concludes that legislators should not have discretion to weigh all factors case-by-case. They do their job best by regarding freedom as uncompromisable, by refusing across the board to undercut freedom of choice and liberty for those who are most immedi-

---

[64] Rolf Sartorius, "The Enforcement of Morality," *Yale Law Journal,* **81**, 891 (1972). Sartorius offers the argument for consideration but is aware of some of its problems and defects. This is not his final view of the matter.

[65] Hart makes a similar argument on the particular point in Chapter 3 of *Law, Liberty, and Morality.*

ately involved in controversial activities. This version of rule-utilitarianism thus sets a rule that restricts the legislator's weighing of benefit and harm, and it does so in the interest of achieving most benefit and harm overall.

Several assumptions in this argument are vulnerable. The first presupposes that a legislator can distinguish the *class* of controversial cases governed by the rule to favor liberty absolutely from the class of noncontroversial cases. But how does one decide whether persons engaged in an unpopular activity are involved in a significant exercise of freedom? Weighing is inescapable; to see whether a religious ritual in which persons are willingly maimed is, say, more like free speech than battery, one must weigh the relevance of liberty *before* one can apply the rule, before one can know whether this activity is properly in the protected class of controversial cases.

There is a serious difficulty with the third point as well. Are legislators generally predisposed to undervalue liberty? To be sure, groups favoring limitations on liberty are often vocal and influential. But the relaxation of restrictive laws is also often favored by altruistic groups formed to support civil liberties or by groups likely to profit directly from such relaxation. A legislator's response to influences will depend on his own values and experiences. Can we assume out of hand that the typical legislator will undervalue liberty or lack resilience in the face of pressure for repressive legislation? The third assumption seems context dependent, its correctness varying from situation to situation.

The fourth point, that there can be no standard for sorting out controversial cases, is implausibly broad. Surely one can chip away at the problem as legislators have always done; they have not always been unsuccessful in deciding what to do about particular situations. They can make informed guesses about the relative impact of limitations on speech and expression, on sexual activity, and so on, and they can create provisional rules.[66] The resulting practice is midway between the weighing test (Devlin's repaired position) and the use of an absolute rule for controversial cases involving liberty. It is hard to see why such an intermediate position is untenable.

Dworkin offers an alternative argument that is a persuasive reconstruction of Mill.[67] Let's begin consideration of it by recalling why it seemed that the overall purpose of a legal system would be to benefit persons and minimize harm. Why is it inappropriate to single out some persons for benefit and not others; why not disregard the harm that some suffer? The answer may seem obvious, but it points to an important feature of moral discourse and moral experience as we have come to conceive of it in Western culture. We presuppose that in moral decisions all persons are entitled to equal respect and concern.[68] To regard persons in this way is not only to take each person seriously as a recipient of benefit and victim of harm, but also to take seriously each person's preferences for how to live and how to realize ideals. To treat others with equal concern and respect is *not* to distribute benefits and suffering in equal shares, but to distribute them in such a way that each person is best able to realize a personal conception of the good life.[69]

---

[66] The formulation of such intermediate rules is not easier in kind from the job of formulating very general principles but only easier in degree. There will, of course, be unresolvable controversies. Compare note 56.

[67] Compare Mill's response to Stephen, described above.

[68] The argument for this is made in *Taking Rights Seriously,* particularly in Chapters 7, 9, 11–13. See also Dworkin, "No Right Answer?," in Joseph Raz and Peter Hacker (eds.), *Law, Morality, and Society* (Oxford, 1977). In reconstructing Dworkin's argument, I am drawing on discussions held by Ronald Dworkin at a National Endowment for Humanities seminar in jurisprudence in Cambridge, Massachusetts, in July and August 1978.

[69] Dworkin, *Taking Rights Seriously,* p. 227.

This notion needs much clarification because the notion of equal respect is abstract and because hard questions force us to define its nature and limits. Recall that what we are after is an alternative to the weighing test (the repaired Devlin theory) that says that liberty is to be weighed alongside other benefits case-by-case in determining when and how to legislate. In Sartorius's argument we have the rule-utilitarian alternative, which instructs legislators to favor liberty whenever expressions of liberty are seriously threatened because they would do the weighing badly with irreparable damage to liberty. In contrast, Dworkin's theory steps back from the debate to ask how either argument is generated in the first place. He concludes that any weighing of benefits and harms is an activity that presupposes not liberty but equality, the equal entitlement of persons to have aspirations, benefits, and harms taken seriously. The imperative to maximize particular liberties over a broad range is one consequence of that supposition.[70] If liberty is understood in this way, Dworkin argues, we can give the legislator a tool for distinguishing a demand for liberty as freedom to impose a particular way of life on others (or harm oneself) from liberty as independence to choose how one will live.[71] We have seen that, in other words, the legislator must distinguish personal preferences, which are the expressions of personal ideals and hopes, from external preferences, which are expressions of desires to limit the pursuit of personal ideals by others.

Two consequences, which I shall not be able to explore, are that Dworkin's theory yields both a way of distinguishing liberalism and conservatism as political theories and a defense of liberalism.[72] Liberalism, in

[70] Ibid., pp. 272-278.
[71] Ibid., pp. 262-263.
[72] This is drawn from Chapter 11 of *Taking Rights Seriously,* from the seminar discussions (note 68), and from "Liberalism" published in Stuart Hampshire (ed.), *Public and Private Morality* (Cambridge, 1979).

this view, is a political theory based on the assumption of equal concern and respect for each person's independence and ideals. According to a liberal theory, it is never a good argument for laws that a *limitation* of options will make one's life better against one's will. What *is* available is the argument that a law will affect one's options to allow one to develop and pursue comprehensive and satisfying life plans.[73] In a conservative theory, changes that are likely to make society better are *pro tanto* justified whether they increase *or* restrict opportunities to form and act out independent life plans.

The implicit argument for liberalism follows simply. It is that *unless* persons respect the independence of others in the way liberalism demands, they are violating a condition of all moral reasoning and experience, that one not favor oneself and one's own preferences but regard others and their preferences as entitled to the same respect one accords oneself. Thus, Dworkin's response to the problem of the morality of legislation parallels Mill. Both see the injunction to weigh all relevant benefits and harms, including liberty, as incomplete. (This is equally relevant as criticism of Stephen and of his intellectual heir, Devlin.) In private moral discourse it may be pointless to make explicit that others are entitled to equal respect. The reason is that individual moral acts rarely affect liberty or the distribution of benefits over large numbers of persons. A political or legislative decision usually has such effects. In judicial decisions it is also otiose to insist that judges

---

[73] One difficulty with the distinction is that an action that enriches the field of possibilities in one respect may impoverish it in others. A decision to subsidize regional theater is at the same time a decision not to use the same resources to subsidize some other cultural activity. Dworkin would say that this does not deny someone an option out of a conviction that his life can be made better in certain ways. Although no existing option is terminated in the imagined case, the distinction between the decision not to create an option and the decision to terminate an existing option may be an insignificant difference.

must have respect for those affected by their decisions.[74] In cases of individual and judicial decisions, therefore, an account of moral decision as a weighing of benefits and harms seems roughly adequate. When we come to the distinctive job of making laws, however, it is important to identify the principle of equal respect, which *explains* why benefit and harm need to be weighed *and* why the independence of persons has special importance.

It is unfair to assess Dworkin's theory using this synopsis. In his book *Taking Rights Seriously,* he applies the theory to hard cases of legislative and judicial decisions. This brief account does, however, let us compare his theory with those of Devlin and Sartorius and see what open questions would have to be answered. Dworkin's theory, as we have seen, has this advantage over Devlin's repaired theory: it shows that a legislative decision differs from an ordinary weighing of benefits (in individual moral reasoning) because it is likely to affect the opportunities of persons for self-realization. Sartorius, like Dworkin, stresses the importance of liberty, the importance of a legal framework in which attempts at self-realization are encouraged and respected. But Sartorius seems to find a solution with only the illusion of simplicity. The problems of deciding case-by-case when and how seriously liberty is threatened remain. Dworkin would be the first to admit that his own theory, without pretensions of simplicity, leaves much for the legislator or judge to do. It is hard, as we have seen, to tell a personal choice or preference from a so-called external preference; a preference about how others should live is often at the same time a preference not to have one's familiar social environment damaged. Dworkin gives insufficient attention to this overlap. Moreover, to acknowl-

[74] See Chapter 2, pages 107–118.

edge that persons are entitled to equal respect and concern is not yet to produce a theory of rights for deciding hard cases. As Dworkin himself shows, a decision in a hard case is always an examination of the moral expectations and opportunities embodied in our legal system, applied to the facts of the case. It is hard to see how the legislator can avoid a weighing, in which rights receive special attention. The weighing of factors determines whether persons have the sorts of rights that can act as trumps on the sort of laws or decisions that would undercut them.

Paternalism

In the last section we looked at several ways of taking account of two goals of law that often conflict, securing liberty as independence and protecting persons from harm caused by others. We have examined how Mill and Stephen, Devlin and Dworkin analyze the job of legislative decision in terms of these broad goals. This is a simplification, because there is a third goal that often affects legislative decisions. Persons may not only harm each other; they may also harm themselves. Legislation that attempts to prevent persons from harming themselves is paternalistic legislation. Paternalistic laws may be designed not only to prevent self-harm but also to bring about self-benefit. An example of the first is a law forbidding the use of intoxicants; an example of the second is a law making education compulsory.

Very few laws are exclusively paternalistic in the sense that their only justification is to keep persons from harming themselves. Most paternalistic laws have some nonpaternalistic justification because a self-harming act is likely to have harmful secondary effects on others. Laws controlling the use of addictive intoxicants may protect the families or dependents of those who would become addicts or the taxpaying public, which has an interest in keeping persons from becoming public charges. The same can be said for laws designed to bring about safe driving, to restrict access to dangerous sports, and so on. Therefore, we have to be careful in examining laws for which the prevention of self-harm plays *some* part in their justification. We can distinguish (a) laws for which nonpaternalistic reasons are *sufficient* to justify a restriction or requirement from (b) laws for which nonpaternalistic justifications are not sufficient. The second class is of interest because it forces us to examine when, if ever, paternalistic reasons justify laws.

The various protagonists of the debate just discussed have anticipatable views on paternalism. Mill argues that paternalistic laws are almost never justified, that "the only purpose for which power can be rightfully exercised over any member of a civilized community, against his will, is to prevent harm to others. His own good, either physical or moral, is not a sufficient warrant. He cannot rightfully be compelled to do or forbear because it will be better for him to do so, because it will make him happier, because, in the opinion of others, to do so would be wise, or even right."[75] Mill qualifies this in two ways. Those who are unable to take care of themselves and make choices for themselves (children, the severely retarded) need to be cared for and protected from harming themselves. Moreover, Mill approves the paternalistic use of nonlegal means to urge others to lead better lives. He endorses moral criticism and moral education to improve the range of choices available to persons and increase the likelihood that each will choose well. He takes note of the informal sanction of "loss of consideration which a person may

[75] *On Liberty*, Chapter 1.

rightly incur by defect of prudence or of personal dignity."[76]

Although Devlin's response to Mill is not made as a paternalistic argument, it has paternalistic implications. Mill's position requires one to distinguish acts that harm others from acts that primarily harm the actor. Devlin seems to challenge the possibility of doing this. He argues that the long-term effects of acts that affect the actor in the first instance will be to change the way of life of all by changing attitudes and affronting feelings. There are really two arguments here. The first is that most acts that *seem* to harm only the actor will in fact harm others by damaging the fabric of society; this is inevitable when persons do not live in permanent isolation. The second argument is that there is no sound reason not to keep others from harming themselves. If one is convinced that an act freely chosen is seriously harmful to the actor, there can be no better reason for intervening. Although there may be practical reasons for doing nothing in particular cases,[77] there is no general principle against intervention. In this view there is no "critical morality" like Mill's according to which all paternalistic interventions against acts of competent adults are impermissible.[78]

Dworkin would be likely to respond to Devlin's second point, his general defense of paternalism, by reiterating that to have equal respect and concern for persons is to have respect for their capacity to live independent lives. This is incompatible with Devlin's unqualified endorsement of paternalism. It is compati-

[76] Ibid., Chapter 4.

[77] Such practical reasons would include, for example, the reason that enforcement would require excessive expenditures of time or manpower and would be inefficient.

[78] Compare Stephen's remarks, note 38, and accompanying text. Compare also Hart's insistence on the need to distinguish between critical and positive morality, note 60, and accompanying text.

ble with the judgment that they could be given the
opportunity to lead better lives, but it "trumps" the
suggestion that they can be coerced into making better
choices.[79] This argument also has two strands. The first
is that we must be humble in forcing on others our
personal sense of what it is to live well. One must not
assume that what works in the context of one life and
one personal history will also work in a different life.
The other strand is that even when we feel confident
that A would be better off doing . . . , this is the judgment that A would be better off if A *chose* to do. . . .
A would not be better off, in many but not all cases,
if compelled to . . . , because this would be an incursion
on the supervening values of independence and choice.

To examine Dworkin's theory let's look at examples of paternalistic legislation, looking first at the
exceptions which even Mill accepted. Mill said that
paternalistic laws are justifiable to protect children
and incompetents. The justification is in the form of
a hypothetical argument: if the child had sufficient
maturity and experience, it would wish to have the
benefits conferred by such legislation. It would wish,
for example, to be taken away from parents who were
mistreating it or to be forced to go to school. Thus,
the actual objections of children to such measures are
seen differently from the choices of an adult. In a
sense, the hypothesis can be confirmed. Legislators who
make such decisions are children who have grown up;
they can recall similar changes of attitude in their own
experience. A similar argument is used to justify paternalistic laws protecting those who are temporarily
incapacitated. The confirmable hypothesis is that, after
recovering, they would wish to have been treated in
a way that protects their interests and assures recovery.
The same kind of justification for treating severely
retarded persons has an obvious, but not fatal, flaw.

[79] This is taken largely from Dworkin's discussions; see note 68.

The argument that such persons would wish to have their interests taken care of in a certain way is in principle not confirmable; the retarded person, unlike the child or the injured, will never be in a position to say responsibly that we have guessed right.

This form of justification is persuasive with regard to children and to the temporarily and permanently incapacitated. Their states are such that they need guardians. But there are additional problems. The argument presumes that there is a consensus about what *is* in the best interests of those being protected, and that there is a consensus about what society's stake is in their welfare.[80] But it may be hard to know what is best: consider, for example, the rights and benefits involved in the question whether and under what circumstances school-age children may be educated at home. A second difficulty is the definition of incapacity. One may limit its application to uncontroversial cases—children, the unconscious, the severely retarded. According to this interpretation, it is primarily a distinction of status and there are relatively distinct boundaries. One can establish by law an age at which the disability of being a child ceases; one can create tests for minimal mental competence.[81] On the other hand, one may extend the notion of incapacity in two ways: one may say that anyone is in a state of incapacity if he or she is in a particular condition *or* if he or she seeks to do a certain thing. For example, one may say that anyone who is in a state of intoxication or drug addiction is incapacitated for purposes of paternalistic legislation *or* one may say that anyone who wants to commit suicide is in a state of incapacity.

[80] See, for example, Joseph Goldstein et al., *Beyond the Best Interests of the Child* (New York, 1974).

[81] There are problems even here. The age of legal maturity may have to be set at different levels for such different activities as drinking and driving; it will not be equally appropriate to persons who develop and mature at different rates; and it will have to be changed as general patterns of maturation change.

I shall call such extensions of the incapacity justification *"per se* rules," rules to the effect that a condition
or desire is *per se* evidence of incapacity. Such rules
can easily be abused to impose one's own preferences.
It could be said that anyone who wishes to engage in
homosexual behavior is thereby demonstrating incapacity. This could even be said of persons who prefer
classical to rock music, or Chinese food to French. One
person's choice may be another's sign of incapacity,
making him or her fit for paternalistic control. In this
extreme form the argument moves from "I do not wish
to do *x*" to "I do not see how anyone could reasonably
want to do *x*" to "It is not a violation of anyone's freedom to forbid persons to do *x*." This argument is an
abuse of power and of logic when *x* is itself not particularly harmful to the actor (eating anchovies for dessert)
or when its harmfulness is at best a matter of controversy and doubt (homosexual behavior). But it also an
abuse when *x* is clearly risky or harmful (driving motor-
cycles, eating foods with cholesterol). To forbid persons
to engage in all activities that are likely to be harmful
to some extent is to constrain choice beyond the
practice of most totalitarian governments.

If the *per se* rule is too broad, the status classification
rule is too narrow. Let's use the notion of equal respect
to show this. To show equal respect for others is to
show respect for their preferences as evidence of their
choices among ways of living one's life. One may en-
rich their options, for example, by subsidizing cultural
programs, but one may not impose choices on them.
This is true even when their choices are likely to harm
them. This general position on paternalistic legislation,
which seems to be Dworkin's, begs the question of the
meaning of equal respect.[82] It assumes that "equal
respect" means both (a) taking benefits to others as

---

[82] We postponed this question at the end of the section, "Theories of
Liberty and Equal Respect."

seriously as I take benefits to myself *and* (b) respecting the self-harming choices of others and according them the same deference as I accord my own choices. I shall argue that there are good arguments for accepting (a) and questioning (b).

Part of my (or anyone's) self-understanding is that I sometimes make uninformed or badly informed choices and that others are sometimes more expert in making some judgments for me than I am myself. I am also aware that I make some choices irrationally—out of anger, frustration, false hope, and so on. To be sure, it is important to me to make some of these mistakes, important because making mistakes is inseparable from having independence and because some consequences simply cannot be anticipated. But this is not true of all my mistakes, nor is it true that my autonomy depends on being able to make every kind of self-harming mistake. Thus, it seems to me, no simple policy toward paternalistic laws follows from the principle of equal concern and respect. The principle seems to involve (b_1) respecting some of the self-harming choices of others, namely those that are part of a rational life plan. This is a much weaker principle than (b). In accord with (b_1) it follows that decisions about the need for particular paternalistic laws depend on a determination of several things: (1) the seriousness and certainty of the particular harms involved, (2) the likelihood that uninformed decisions about such acts will be made, (3) the likelihood that such decisions will not be made rationally, (4) the relative importance of such acts in the lives of those who are likely to choose to do them, and (5) the difficulty and nature of practical means of enforcing such laws.[83] It follows that even though the *per se* rule is likely to be used too broadly, the point

[83] These suggestions are offered by Gerald Dworkin, "Paternalism," in Richard Wasserstrom (ed.), *Morality and the Law* (Belmont, Calif., 1971). For another illuminating discussion of paternalism, see Joel Feinberg, "Legal Paternalism," *Canadian Journal of Philosophy,* 1, 105 (1971).

of it makes some sense. It is that individuals are less informed and less rational in some choices than in others; to the extent that legislators believe that no informed person could rationally choose to do himself or herself harm of a particular kind and severity, they are morally justified in supporting paternalistic intervention.

If all this is correct, the legislator must go beyond status classification to protect responsible persons from *some* risks. He must make particular judgments about the various kinds of harm individuals may inflict on themselves using the factors just listed.[84] There are no "right" answers to questions about paternalistic legislation unless there are "right" answers about how these factors are to be weighed in particular cases. Let's consider special problems raised by each factor in turn.

(1) Paternalistic laws are justified only to protect persons against considerable and irreversible (or hard to reverse) harm. On the one hand, harm may be physical (laws prohibiting suicide, requiring the use of motorcycle helmets, prohibiting the use of addictive intoxicants, or forbidding dueling or swimming at public beaches in the absence of lifeguards). Such physical harm may be immediate (suicide) or delayed (the cumulative effects of smoking), certain (suicide) or a statistical risk (motorcycle injury). On the other hand, the harm may be economic (laws requiring persons to buy retirement annuities, forbidding usury) or psychological (laws prohibiting gambling or forbidding child labor). Laws against gambling and child labor are justified as preventing several kinds of harm at once.

Because serious harm is a necessary factor, to disagree about the severity or likelihood of harm is to disagree about the desirability of such legislation. Laws

[84] See note 82.

restricting forms of sexual conduct for paternalistic reasons are good examples of laws based on much disputed psychological theories.

(2) Once serious harm is shown, a question that is relevant to the desirability of legal protection is whether ignorance accounts for the risk, whether one may eliminate the danger simply by publicizing it. If so, more invasive public action is undesirable. But in all the examples we might consider (motorcycle helmets, suicide, drug and alcohol addictions, dueling, usury, child labor, gambling) ignorance is not the main problem. If usury is partially an exception, then "truth-in-lending" laws are a solution. In most of the other cases, the participant has been warned of the harmful consequences and still runs the risk.

(3) It next becomes important to consider whether such persons can be said to act rationally on the knowledge they are presumed to have. The test, on first impression, is easy. Addicts, whether addicted to drugs, alcohol, or gambling, are thought to be unable to choose rationally and driven by inner compulsion; the victims of usury cannot act in their long-term best interests because of short-term financial peril. Would-be suicides are said to suffer under internal or external pressures that prevent rational decisions. On the other hand, those who choose to use nonaddictive drugs, to play dangerous sports, or to do without motorcycle helmets are making rational choices about what matters most to them. The difficulty with these conclusions is that they rest on cliché. Is rationality so clear a concept?

One problem is that *all* choices are made under some external constraints and some psychological predispositions. The decision to duel or to play a dangerous sport may be the acting out of a self-destructive impulse or a response to peer pressure, an appeal for respect or acceptance. Or, a decision to gamble, which may

seem compulisve to a legislator who cannot imagine
the thrill of risk-taking, *may* be as freely made as any
other choice of entertainment. Furthermore, if we
generally allow persons to make even ruinous bargains,
what is distinctive about usury that we assume that
persons *could* not choose to pay very high interest
rates for a short-term loan?

Notwithstanding these substantial difficulties, the
distinction may be defended. Consider again the hypothetical question, what would the actor have chosen
if she or he had been capable of choice? The hypothesis
may be answered and the absence of capacity may be
established after the fact; the recovered addict but not
the inveterate risk-taker can confirm that he or she has
been helped by paternalistic protection. This test helps
sort out cases of would-be suicides, a class that is
particularly heterogeneous because the term refers not
to a situation but simply to a sought consequence.
There is a need to distinguish the temporarily deranged
would-be suicide (the rejected lover perhaps) from the
terminally ill person. The task of the legislator is thus
to frame rules in anticipation of such results, rules
that distinguish cases of genuine choice, even under
constraint, from cases in which inner and outer circumstances take the power of choice away. If the job is
extraordinarily difficult, the distinction and the need
to use it are unavoidable.

(4) A distinction that parallels and reinforces the
point just made is between potentially self-harming
acts that are part of a possible life plan and those
that interrupt or disrupt the pursuit of such a plan.
Again this is a way of distinguishing among various
forms of suicide, of distinguishing the person who
wishes to die with dignity from the person who wishes
to punish others by killing him- or herself.

(5) Still another factor in determining paternalistic
laws is enforcement. Paternalistic laws are unlike other

laws in a way that creates a unique problem for enforcement. The persons they are designed to protect
are themselves trying to evade the laws. The legislator
must consider whether the available means of enforcement are (a) effective enough to bring about compliance, (b) likely to "chill" liberty in ways that are too
costly, and (c) likely to corrupt the enforcers and
others. Laws that make it mandatory to wear motorcycle helmets illustrate the first problem. Evasion is
easy and widespread; enforcement doesn't seem worth
the cost in work-hours and effective penalties seem too
harsh. The second and third problems are illustrated in
enforcing laws against kinds of sexual conduct, gambling, or drug use. The enforcement of such laws usually
invades liberty—free speech, association, privacy. Enforcement depends on the use of informers, undercover
agents, and wiretapping and it is argued that such
strategies so corrupt the police and their agents that
the costs are too great. Such laws may also lead to
entrapment, cases in which the initiative for the offense
originates with the enforcement officer.

We have addressed the issue of paternalism as if
paternalistic reasons were the primary ones for having
drugs laws, laws against child labor or usury, laws
against gambling, or laws requiring motorcycle helmets.
Such activities usually involve the risk of secondary
harm to others; nonpaternalistic reasons will be available to justify such legislation, often decisively. Also,
we have assumed that the only way of affecting such
categories of activity is by forbidding them. Of course,
many means are available. It is possible to discourage
consumption of a harmful substance (cigarettes, for
example) by taxing its use; the effect will depend on
how elastic the demand for the product is. Taxes also
have the effect of making the product unavailable only
to those unable to pay the added price. Alternatively,
laws have indirect paternalistic effects when they

punish the producers or sellers rather than the consumers of harmful substances, and when they license and regulate production and sale. Still other means that are sometimes usable are to provide attractive alternatives to the harmful activity.

The issues raised by paternalism resist summation in a principle that can be used to make hard cases easy. The point of my analysis, here as elsewhere, was to see why hard cases are hard. These examples again point out the special sensitivity and care that the lawmaker must exercise in restricting liberty, in making laws that threaten to limit opportunities to make personally satisfying choices and act upon them. At the same time, no principle prohibiting interference with liberty and no formulaic account of rights are likely to help solve hard cases.

Conclusions and Open Questions

My purpose has been to clarify some debates about morality and legislation. Such debates are often about a pseudo-problem, the problem whether law ought to be the enforcement of morals. To be sure, the legislator's job is to set rules of governance that are likely to most benefit persons governed by such rules and to minimize harm to them. To say this is only to describe the framework of debate. Devlin's first position in this debate is that law exists to implement a consensus in the attitudes of persons toward their own interests. But this position assumes that such a consensus exists and ignores the disparate reasons why persons have the attitudes they do have. The legislator's wisdom is, in part, to recognize the possibility of oppression by government in the name of consensus, and to recognize the inevitable costs of coercing by law any form of behavior. Thus, the legislator must seek to find a zone of noninterference, in which persons are most benefited by being left to their own preferences and damaged by being compelled to act in accord with the preferences of others. At this point the debate becomes one about the most reasonable and coherent justification for recognizing autonomy and independence, the most reasonable theory for the legislator to have in mind in making laws. According to one theory, liberty is one of several benefits to be conferred on persons, or denied, on a case-by-case basis. By another theory, liberty (as the exercise of rights) is a "trump" over decisions to implement other benefits through law because it can be derived from the moral presumption that each person is to be treated with equal respect and concern. Such theories ultimately differ as pictures of the kind of society in which it is best to live. They assign different value to self-determination. This difference leads to different prescriptions for weighing the exercise of rights against other benefits. In addition, Dworkin's theory suggests that we have inherited a moral commitment to equality, to equal respect and concern for others, which must underlie any allocation of benefits. Neither theory has the advantage of absolving the legislator of responsibility for evaluating ambiguous consequences and making hard choices. Finally, a legislator's commitment to take seriously the preferences of persons must be tempered and honed in decisions about paternalistic laws. Here the temptation to impose preferences is most immediate and direct.

4

Responsibility and Punishment

•

Voluntariness and Choice

The problems we examined in Chapters 1 through 3 are all about law as decision-making. We looked at judges and legislators as decision-makers and looked for critical standards with which to evaluate such decisions. The obedience or disobedience of citizens also reflects decisions. When Hart says that law is a system of rules he is saying that law is pervaded with decision-making: law is a system of rules that certain persons have devised, that may be changed by prescribed procedures, and that are designed to be understood and followed conscientiously by those who are subject to them.

The conceptual link between law and decision-making is especially clear in criminal law. A basic commitment of criminal law as we know it is that persons shall be subject to criminal penalties only if they have had an opportunity to obey and have nevertheless disobeyed. It is not enough to do what the law forbids; punishment is appropriate only for those who have chosen to disobey. This requirement for criminal liability is described by the Latin phrase, *mens rea,* which means "guilty mind." Later in this chapter we will examine the contours and limitations of this notion.

Decision-making is not only an important concept in law, it is also a confusing and complex one. It belongs to a family of concepts that philosophers have always found difficult to define or explain, concepts such as volition, will, intention, action, choice, and responsibility. These concepts are as important in moral evaluation as they are in law. Moral blame, like legal liability, is thought to be appropriate for persons who can choose to comply with rules, who act intentionally, and who are therefore responsible (morally or legally) for what they do.

Several branches of philosophy—philosophy of mind, philosophical psychology, and philosophy of action[1] — are all concerned with the aspects of human nature to which these concepts refer. Writings in these areas describe the nature and relationship of thought, feeling, and action. Although we cannot survey this extensive literature, we must look at part of it, the part that spells out the underpinnings of any system of rules and responsibility. There are several reasons why such an examination is essential.

(1) Many persons believe, and many writers have argued, that all talk about decision-making and choice rests on a myth about human nature. This belief takes many forms. Some persons argue that all behavior is necessarily determined by one's perceptions about

---

[1] See, for example, Donald Gustafson (ed.), *Essays in Philosophical Psychology* (Garden City, N.Y., 1964); Alan White (ed.), *The Philosophy of Action* (Oxford, 1968); Stuart Hampshire, *Thought and Action* (London, 1959); and Norman Malcolm, *Problems of Mind* (New York, 1971).

what is in one's self-interest. In this view, no one is capable of acting or choosing to act in any other way. Another argument says that we use notions like choice and decision-making to conceal our ignorance of the determinants of behavior. If we had more adequate psychological theories and if we fitted these theories to the particular histories of individuals, we would see that their behavior was necessitated by their history and personality. Still another argument for the same conclusion is that the laws of physiology and biochemistry will eventually give us an understanding of human behavior in which we will be able to predict human action and see that choice is an illusion.

All these so-called deterministic arguments entail that the notions of choice and decision-making rest on a mistake. If this were true, it would (it seems) require us to change the ways in which we think of ourselves quite radically. We have seen that every description we make of moral situations and moral responsibility rests on the concepts of choice and decision; every account we give of judging or legislating presupposes that it makes sense to speak of choice. The concepts of a rule and of following a rule, which positivists use as the fulcrum of their account of law, are intelligible only if there is choice. Machines and plants are incapable of disobedience and, therefore, of obedience; persons, we say, can obey because they can choose to disobey.[2] It is important to see whether moral and legal thinking are in this way based on a myth.

(2) In law in general, but particularly in criminal law, we are concerned not only with saying that persons make choices and have intentions but also with saying

---

[2] I am not using the phrase "following a rule" in the sense in which the carrying out of a natural process is the following of a rule. I am concerned, in other words, with obedience and not with the operation of laws of nature.

that one person can know what another's intentions
are. Punishing depends on deciding that offenders intended to do harm. Often the degree of punishment
is made proportional to the degree of harm intended.

Some philosophers have claimed, however, that persons can never know the intentions of others. Surveying
the general categories of what can be known, they
conclude that we can only know our own private feelings and thoughts and those things that are in the
publicly observable physical world.[3] The feelings,
thoughts, or intentions of others are private to them
and only they have "privileged access."

This philosophical argument has the general form of
a skeptical argument. This means that it takes up a distinction made in everyday thought, in this case the
distinction between another person's intended and
unintended actions, and tries to show that the distinction is logically untenable and must be given up. It
does this by taking and arguing for a position on the
nature and limits of knowledge. To meet the skeptic's
arguments, we will have to challenge the skeptical
account of knowledge. And we *must* do so if we are
to be able to explain our ability to make the judgments about intentions that are one of the bases of
criminal law and law in general.

(3) Once we have shown that the notions of choice,
decision, and intention can be defended against these
various philosophical attacks, we must see just *how*
they are used within law (and within morality). This
is a considerable job, and we can only do a small part
of it. For example, there are many ways in which law
and morality diverge. We shall see why, for the most
part, legal judgments are made on the basis of a person's
intentions but not motives, whereas moral judgments

[3] For a dialogue on the subject of the possibility of knowing other
minds see A. J. Ayer, "One's Knowledge of Other Minds," and Norman
Malcolm, "Knowledge of Other Minds," both of which are reprinted in
Gustafson, op. cit., note 1.

take both intention and motive into account. We shall also see why the law sometimes declines to look at the intentions of offenders at all and *imputes* to them an intention even when it is not present.

The role that *moral* blameworthiness (or fault) plays in the formulation of *legal* standards is complex. In general, the thresholds for attributing moral responsibility and legal responsibility are the same: persons are held responsible for their intentional conduct, for what they choose to do. More broadly, they are responsible for behavior over which they can be expected to have had control. This broader account allows us to include responsibility for reckless or negligent conduct that may not be intentional but that is, one usually assumes, subject to the actor's control. But there are divergences, cases in which those who are morally at fault are not at fault in the eyes of the law and cases in which persons are punished but are morally blameless. These divergences can usually be explained by looking at the special purposes and limitations of law as an institution. We shall see whether a utilitarian account of the purposes of law can help us to do so.

Criminal law needs a special kind of moral examination and justification. In criminal cases, the state (or society) is the plaintiff. Criminal law is therefore concerned not with adjusting the rights and obligations of contending individuals but with enforcing the rights of society against the individual. The basis of criminal law, unlike some other branches of law, is that society has the right to punish by inflicting harm on persons because of their conduct. This sets a problem for a utilitarian way of thinking, because the inflicting of harm is justifiable only if it is a necessary part of achieving some greater benefit. A utilitarian account of the justification of criminal punishment would have to satisfy three challenges. Each challenge has the form of saying that utilitarianism cannot adequately explain the institution of punishment.

The first challenge is based on the observation that the punishment ought to be limited to those who are blameworthy and intend to do the harm that they bring about. The challenge is that a utilitarian could not justify this criterion for punishment because punishing the blameworthy is not justified unless there is compensatory benefit and because punishing or harming those who are not blameworthy may be justified when there *is* compensatory benefit. The second challenge follows from the first. It is that a utilitarian would determine the nature and degree of punishment solely by looking at the goal of achieving greatest overall benefit, whereas the practice in criminal law is often to let the degree of blameworthiness determine the nature and degree of punishment. The last challenge is the farthest reaching one. It says that a utilitarian scheme of justification would allow the state to invade the life of an individual in a beneficial *or* harmful way whenever the most beneficial results overall can be advanced by doing so. This, it is said, camouflages the special nature of criminal law. The acts and intentions of the criminal *allow* the state to invade his life and punish accordingly; a scheme of justification must explain both the ordinary invulnerability of persons to such invasions and the special vulnerability of the criminal. In the last sections of this chapter I shall discuss the justification of punishment with special attention to whether utilitarianism can meet these challenges.

There are, we have seen, several reasons why an examination of the foundations of law must answer some questions raised in the philosophy of mind and action. These questions are all questions about the concept of responsibility, a concept that links psychology and moral theory by identifying the psychological presuppositions that underlie moral judgment (and legal judgment).

Determinism

The debate over free will and determinism is one of the oldest in philosophy. It begins with the observation that the habit of thinking of oneself as having free will is deeply ingrained in human nature. All thoughts about choice, decision, and responsibility are based on the assumption of free will. At the same time (it is said), the more we find out about human nature through science, the more the assumption that there is such a thing as free will conflicts with other closely held and well-based beliefs.

This incompatibility is explained in the following way. The progress of scientific knowledge is progress in being able to give causal explanations; we come to understand events better as we come to know their causes. In the world of everyday experience all events are caused and the idea of an uncaused or free event is an absurdity.[4] (Philosophers have made this point in various ways. Hume said that persons inevitably form the habit of thinking in causal terms. Kant said that causation was one of the categories through which the understanding operates.)[5]

As we learn to explain events causally, we learn to predict and control them. To know that certain conditions are sufficient to cause an event is to be able to predict with certainty that the event will occur. If one can manipulate the antecedent conditions, one can bring about the event. Prediction and control will obviously be easier in some fields than others, easier in chemistry than in history because chemical events can

---

[4] Aristotle, in his *Metaphysics,* discusses the notion of an uncaused causer or "first cause," a concept that has obvious analogies to some notions of God.

[5] See David Hume, *A Treatise of Human Nature,* various editions, Book I, Part III, Section II; Immanuel Kant, *The Critique of Pure Reason,* Transcendental Analytic, Chapter 2.

be isolated and duplicated by experiment. But in all fields the principle of explanation is the same: to understand events is to understand them as parts of determinate causal chains.

It is clear why someone who holds this general view of causal explanation and of the explainability of all events would reject the notion of free will. He sees the doctrine of free will as the doctrine that when persons choose or decide to act, and do so freely, their actions are not in turn caused by anything else. Persons are uncaused causers. The determinist points out, in opposing this conclusion, that there is no reason to think that human action is exempt from causal explanation. In fact, it is explainable from several different perspectives; biochemistry, physiology, psychology, and sociology are only some of the sciences that involve the prediction and/or the control of human behavior.

The determinist also points out that the doctrine of free will is ambiguous. Does it say that free will is a universal feature of all human action? If so, it does not describe the way in which the term is used. In moral and legal reasoning, we distinguish continually between responsible and excusable behavior. Is it the view that only *some* behavior is free? If so, it is hard or impossible to know where the line between free and unfree behavior is drawn. We often find that as we find out more about a person's history and capacities, we take back the assumption that he acted freely. This suggests that the assumption of free acting is usually made in ignorance. The determinist concludes that a symptom of this muddle is that we sometimes speak of an action as being both free and caused. He says that this is inconsistent: to say that an action is free is to say that the actor could have done otherwise; to say it is caused is to say that the actor could not have done otherwise.

This view of determinism is a simplification and it is not any one philosopher's complete argument. It is, however, clear and complete enough to use as a basis for arguing that this kind of determinism breaks down at crucial points and that it does not give us a good reason for abandoning either causal explanation or the notion of free will.

(1) There are many kinds of causal explanation and it is not at all obvious that all kinds fit the determinist's model. Consider some examples from historical explanation. We may say that Nixon's cover-up of the illegal break-in at Watergate caused Nixon's downfall or that the excesses of Louis XVI set in motion the process that led, among other things, to his beheading. Or let's take an example from psychology. An analyst may conclude that a man's marital breakdown was caused by unresolved dependency on his mother. In each case, it is *not* part of the explanation that, other things being equal, the cause necessitated the result. A crisis in foreign affairs might have lead to the postponement of impeachment hearings and have kept Nixon in office. Louis might have escaped from France rather than remain to be beheaded. And the analysand might have remained a meek and submissive husband. The cause is neither a necessary nor a sufficient cause of the outcome. The explanatory link is best described as follows. What is called the cause has a tendency to bring about the result, and it is singled out because it makes the result intelligible by fitting it to a familiar pattern of human experience.

A determinist will respond that we settle for such "weak" explanations because history and human nature are very complicated, because it is hard to conduct experiments, and because events cannot be recreated in all respects. But this only means that we are largely ignorant and have only partial explanations. If we knew much more we would see why things could not have turned out differently.

There are good reasons for remaining unconvinced by the determinist. Consider what we would know if we

assembled all the causes of Nixon's resignation. We
would, first of all, have to name an endless series of
conditions since we would have to exclude every possible event that could have forestalled resignation: the
death of a key senator, a newspaper strike, a foreign
crisis, and so on. It is not clear, moreover, that we could
possibly answer the question that would have to be
asked about every hypothetical condition: Could this
have made a difference? Suppose we do the impossible
and assemble all conditions to arrive at a full causal
explanation that would satisfy the determinist. What
would this tell us? It would tell us that if every prior
event up to the moment of resignation had occurred
just as it did, if there had been no change or intervention whatever, the resignation would also have
occurred. Obviously, this does not give us a general
truth about history *or* insight into Nixon's resignation.
It applies to a single event and tells us something we
already knew, that if Nixon had not resigned, it would
have been a task for historians to explain why. Historians would work to give us a reason that distinguishes
the nonresignation from the resignation. Thus, by
pursuing the determinist's model for causal investigation
and explanation, we have only come up with a general
working principle for historians, that if two events are
different, their causes must be different. This is not a
discovery but a principle of investigation.

All of this suggests that the determinist's model for
explanation does not describe or fit all modes of causal
explanation and fits historical and psychological explanation very badly. Let's see one reason why this is so.
The determinist's goals are satisfied when he can specify
the conditions sufficient for an event. The ideal is deductive: certain premises entail a conclusion. In the
physical sciences, causal explanation often does pursue
this ideal. To take a simple example, Boyle's Law about
the relation of pressure and volume of gases describes
an ideal situation. It assumes that certain features of

a situation can be held constant and can therefore be discounted in formulating the law. It assumes that gases are perfectly elastic, that they are not superheated or supercooled, that the system is closed, and so on. The law is used with the qualification that under *normal conditions* certain causes will yield certain effects. We have a sound intuitive idea of the meaning of "normal conditions" even if it is impossible to specify all the matters that the phrase covers.

We can now see why the same kind of idealization and generalization of events does not occur in historical or psychological explanation.[6] There is usually no answer to the question of what a person or state would do in "normal conditions." To be sure, there are some general propositions. A man who has been starved will probably eat; a state that faces insurrection will try to suppress it. But our ability to formulate these general "laws" is directly related to the fact that they are generally uninformative. In history and psychology, causal explanation becomes informative to the extent that it deals with events that are so complex that one doesn't know which aspects to put aside as "normal conditions." The causal explanation of neurotic behavior is interesting and informative just because there are no deductive laws of the form, "In ordinary conditions, a man who has a domineering mother will. . . ." At best there are tendencies and dispositions investigated in idiosyncratic and unique settings.

I have tried to argue that the determinist's view of causal explanation may not have universal application. To say that certain conditions caused an event is not necessarily to say that they determined the event by making it inevitable. If this is so, it is not necessarily a contradiction to say that A caused B and to say at

---

[6]This is not true of all kinds of psychological explanation. I am thinking here primarily of clinically based forms of explanation, like psychoanalytical theory, and not of various theories propounded by experimental psychologists.

the same time that, given A, B could have been other-wise. I used examples from history and psychology to suggest that this is particularly so when we are dealing with human behavior, the subject matter of morality and law.

(2) The determinist's rejection of free will has three parts: an account of causal explanation, an account of free will, and a demonstration of their incompati-bility. Having considered the first part, we can turn to the second, which tells us that to say that John made a choice or decided to do . . . is to deny that John's actions were caused. Either John is the author of his actions or events outside John caused them.

Let's begin by distinguishing two claims, the claim that an act is free because it has no causal antecedents, because nothing in its history can be used to explain why it occurred, and the claim that an act is free be-cause it is not done under constraint or compulsion. In the first sense, no act is free unless it is wholly gratuitous[7] and in no way a result of the actor's past history and personality. The second sense is entirely familiar; we distinguish between coercion and freedom continually, but we will need to look closely at the notions of constraint and compulsion. Free action in the first sense cannot be explained causally, but free action in the second sense can be explained causally *if* causal explanation is not the same thing as showing necessitation.

When we say that decisions and choices are free, we mean that they are free in the second sense. They are at the same time causally explainable by appeal to, among other things, the dispositions and personal history of the actor. To press the objection at this point, the determinist will have to argue that all be-

---

[7]French novelists in the 1930s and 1940s were fascinated by the prob-lem of trying to describe a wholly gratuitous act. Andre Gide's novel *Lafcadio's Adventures* (*Les Caves Du Vatican*) is a treatment in fiction of this issue.

havior is done under compulsion and constraint. One cannot do this by repeating that all causation is necessitation or that free action is necessarily uncaused. To say this would be simply to reassert what we have already questioned. Language and personal experience tell us that between necessitated behavior and uncaused behavior is a middle ground in which lie choice and decision. We shall see that the determinist must offer new arguments to show that this is an illusion.

Let's look more closely at the middle ground. Even if we put aside the assumptions of the determinist, there is something odd about saying the behavior is both free and caused. Such a claim threatens to tumble us into the contradiction that the actor is and is not the initiator of actions, that he could and could not have done otherwise. How can such difficulties be avoided?

Consider some examples of compelled (unfree) behavior and caused but free behavior to see the distinguishing marks of each. Consider first a paranoiac who avoids trees because he thinks that armed enemies lurk behind them. In contrast, consider the philanthropist who gives half her fortune to charity partly out of sympathy for the poor and ill and partly out of the desire to avoid high taxes. Or consider the ambitious student who actively seeks fellowships and cultivates the friendship of influential professors. What leads us, at least on first impression, to say that the choices of only the first person are compelled and that he lacks the power to choose his actions?

How can we characterize the most obvious difference between free and unfree behavior? The examples suggest that unfree, compulsive behavior involves a kind of fear or psychological conflict that is invariant and overriding. The actor cannot "fine-tune" behavior to meet the demands of particular situations and achieve goals in those situations. Situations that trigger a paranoid response are dominated by that response; the actor's repertoire of responses is limited. We see

him as self-frustrating and would anticipate that he
himself has a sense of self-frustration.

The person whom we would describe as acting freely
adapts his or her behavior to situations. The philanthropist or ambitious student is able to measure each situation
to see whether it is an appropriate one for pursuing
goals. He or she is someone with whom we can reason,
showing that *this* way of achieving goals may be better
than some other way. The goals may be neither ad-
mirable nor within his or her power to change. Whether
one is the sort of person who is able to make decisions
and exercise "free will" is not a matter of whether one
is able to alter one's personality and commitments
wholesale; it is a matter of how one operates within
them. It may well happen that greater acquaintance
with the philanthropist or student would lead us to
think of them as compulsive and unable to adapt their
behavior. This would be so if we came to see that their
actions were largely self-defeating and that their self-
perceptions were largely inaccurate. Judgments about
freedom and compulsion are relative judgments.

These examples show that it is mistaken to say that
unfree behavior has causes that are external to the
actor and that when behavior is free the actor is himself
the cause. The truly compulsive person may *feel*
"driven" but is no more or less "caused" to act than
anyone else. In *any* situation, the causes of action are
both internal and external, both features of the actor's
personality and awareness and features of the situation
in which the actor is placed. There is no paradox in
saying that someone is both the initiator of events and
acting in the context of his dispositions and the external
features of the situation. To say that he is an initiator
is to refer to his ability to respond in ways that are
appropriate to realizing goals in that situation and to
the subjective sense of control and choice that is the
concomitant of acting in this way. Similarly, there is
no paradox in saying that he could have acted other-

wise in the sense that he could have responded to new arguments designed to change his mind and could have perceived a new facet of the situation and responded accordingly, *and* saying that he could not have chosen to do something other than he did "for no reason whatever."

In summary, the determinist has failed to show that the ways in which we think about human action are inconsistent. He has not shown why we cannot give a psychological account of an action, for example, and at the same time say that we are explaining a genuine choice or decision. Moral and legal reasoning make sense only if these ways of thinking are compatible. We explain causally what led an offender to commit a crime, and we use some of the ingredients of our account to determine whether the offender is to be held legally responsible, whether he can be said to have acted freely. I have tried to show how, compatibly with causal explanation, such distinctions are made.

A determinist may concede that our ways of thinking about causation and free will are not incompatible and still argue that they are wrong. I shall briefly consider the merits of three arguments of this kind.

(1) The first argument admits that we have modest goals for explaining human behavior and we do not have general laws of behavior that allow us to predict what persons will do. But, the argument goes, we cannot *know* that such sciences as physiology, biochemistry, cybernetics, and experimental psychology will not overtake our present conception of human nature. If and when they do, we will come to think of human behavior as no more free than the behavior of plants and fallen rocks. Our confidence that causal explanation and free will are compatible is built on ignorance and the belief that that ignorance will last.

Let's examine the possibility that the determinist is anticipating. He would be correct to say that just because I cannot explain when and why the plates of the earth will cause an earthquake at the St. Andreas fault, I am not justified in saying that they have free will. But with regard to earthquakes we know at least what kind of information would allow us to predict such events. We know that we would have to know more about pressure along the fault, the elasticity of land masses, and so on. We do not know very well how to experiment or investigate to find these things out. With regard to human behavior, on the other hand, we do not know what kinds of discoveries would lead us to say that all behavior follows predictive laws and is unfree.

It may seem that discoveries in physiology, neurology, or cybernetics might do the trick. There are serious conceptual obstacles to such an assumption. For example, it is not clear that one can ever predict future neurological states from information about present states. There may be irreducible randomness in brain events. Moreover, there is no particular reason to be confident that we will ever be able to correlate particular neurological states with relatively complex patterns of thought and action. Although it is possible to correlate some experiences of pleasure or to bring about knee jerks by stimulating nerve endings, it may never be possible to correlate a decision to be charitable or even a decision to eat beef rather than veal with particular neural events.[8]

Suppose, for the sake of argument, that these obstacles were overcome. Suppose what may seem unimaginable, that persons could know in advance how they would act in any given situation. They would be like self-conscious billiard balls. For such persons freedom and choice would indeed have no meaning. But we are not in that situation and, as we have seen,

[8] An excellent bibliography of philosophical writings in this area is to be found in Alan Ross Anderson (ed.), *Minds and Machines* (New York, 1964).

we do not even know that that situation is possible. It makes no more sense to give up such notions as decision and choice because they would have no use in a barely imaginable world, than it would for countries to disarm in this world because in a barely imaginable world there may be universal good will.

(2) The determinist may offer quite a different argument. He may say, using the following examples, that we have no consistent bases for saying that actions are free or compelled, that our thinking on these matters is capricious and inconsistent. In the case of the paranoiac we say that his behavior is compulsive even though we cannot predict when he will yield to his fears. On good days, he may risk walking down a tree-lined street; on others, he may stay fearfully at home—and we may be quite unable to predict his actions. On the other hand, we may predict with assurance that a friend will contribute to a neighborhood charity as she has done for the last thirty years. In these cases we call the less predictable action compulsive and the more predictable one free. The determinist concludes that we have no intelligible criteria.

The determinist is looking for criteria in the wrong place. Let's see why he is arguing in this way. His original claim was that *if* events are causally explainable by laws that demonstrate necessitation, then they are unfree. This is entirely correct, but (as we have seen) human actions are not events of this kind. The determinist assumes incorrectly, however, that if events are *not* causally explainable by laws that demonstrate necessitation, they are free. This does not follow at all. Human actions that are not necessitated are sorted out as being free or unfree on the basis of other criteria. Behavior is free not to the extent that it is predictable or unpredictable but to the extent that the actor can shape behavior in the situation to the achievement of forward-looking goals. The paranoiac's actions are determined by fears that are obstacles to seeking goals;

the benefactor's acts, however regular, are directed toward goals.[9]

(3) A third argument says that we have overlooked a basic "proof" of the incoherence of the notion of free will. All persons act out of self-interest and it would be irrational for them to do otherwise. Persons cultivate the illusion of choice and freedom, but actions are wholly determined by what they think is in their best interest. One can affect behavior by argument but only by changing the actor's opinions about how self-interest is best achieved.

Kant pointed out that moral reasoning presupposes that persons are "autonomous." By this he means that persons must have the capacity to set aside needs and desires, which reflect self-interest, and act for the sake of principles or for the sake of others.[10] While it appears that Kant and determinism are directly opposed, more needs to be said. It would be possible to identify a person's self-interest *with* acting on principle or acting for the sake of others. Such a view would say that persons will necessarily act in ways that will conform with moral action. According to this view there could not possibly be a conflict between self-interest and moral principle, nor could there be cases of sacrificing one's interest for the sake of others.[11] A failure to act in the interest of moral considerations could only be explained as ignorance of where one's real self-interest lay.

The kind of deterministic view that we are examining involves a different and narrower conception of self-interest. It is the ordinary notion whereby it is in one's self-interest to accumulate benefits in the forms of

[9] See this chapter, pp. 187–191.

[10] Immanuel Kant, *Foundations of the Metaphysics of Morals,* Preface and First Section.

[11] The theory that immorality is necessarily based on a kind of ignorance is to be found throughout Plato's writings and is a common feature of much Greek philosophy.

wealth, comfort, and pleasure. In pursuing self-interest, defined in this way, one obviously denies certain benefits to others or competes with them for benefits. For the determinist, it is a myth that persons can do otherwise than pursue whatever they individually regard as most beneficial for them. It is a myth that persons can be autonomous in Kant's sense, a myth that persons can be susceptible to moral arguments and can exercise free choice on the basis of such arguments.

The determinist's position seems to reflect common sense and common expectations. We ordinarily do expect others to act in their own interest as they perceive it. We expect the coherent pattern of their lives to be the realization of personal goals. We think that to do otherwise is irrational. Even if persons find it in their interest sometimes to benefit others, such coincidences of interest are fortuitous. If a person does not already choose to identify his interest with moral or altruistic action, it will be pointless to try to influence him by showing how he will affect others.

This argument seems sensible because it is built on an equivocation. On the one hand, it makes the modest claim that to choose to do something is to prefer to do it, and to prefer to do it is to identify one's interest with doing it. There is a sense in which this is obviously true, but just as obviously it is a limited claim that will not support determinism. Consider the following. A student chooses to take an examination. Therefore, the student prefers to take the examination than to fail the course. One might at the same time prefer to pass the course without being examined but that option is not available. Thus, the first part of the claim must be qualified: to choose is to express a preference, but only among the available options. The second part must also be qualified. An altruist who chooses to give to charity may well have an interest in doing so because the action makes him feel good, or fits in with a self-image and

with values he would like to emulate. But to say that it
is in his interest in this sense is not to say that he *thinks*
of it as being in his interest, or that he does it *because*
it is in his interest, or that he does it for his *own* sake.
All the last points may be false; he may well and correctly think that some interests will suffer because of
his generosity. The question whether his interests overall
are enhanced or diminished is a question we have no
way of answering, a question that may not make much
sense. Thus, the determinist's equivocation is between
saying that persons always get something out of their
choices and actions, even if it is just the satisfaction
of being kind, and saying that persons always act for
the sake of benefiting themselves. The first is true, the
second false. The determinist must be able to demonstrate the second claim to show that persons do not
"really" make choices.

I have used philosophical controversies about determinism and free will as a framework for investigating
the notions of choice and decision-making. These notions are presupposed by any system of rules that
makes consequences to persons turn upon assessments
of responsibility. To understand criminal law it is of
central importance to understand how and why we are
able to distinguish compelled behavior from freely
chosen actions. Criminal law carries forward the task
we have begun here, the task of justifying and applying
criteria for responsibility. We shall continue this investigation in the rest of this chapter.

Skepticism and Other Minds

To understand and accept the notion of legal responsibility, one must not only make sense of the notion of
freely choosing to act. One must also explain how it is
that we are able to tell when others are acting freely.
We have already considered one kind of skeptical argu-

ment that tries to erase the distinction between acting freely and acting under necessitation.[12] Now we must consider a skeptical argument that seeks to erase the distinction between knowing that someone else is acting freely and knowing that they are not.

Suppose Johnson has a motor disability that compels him to kick his left leg forward at random moments. While I am watching, he walks by a sleeping dachshund and kicks it in its hindquarters. What is the difference between Johnson kicking the dog because of his disability and Johnson intentionally kicking the dog? Assume that the physically observable actions are identical. The answer would seem to be that the intentional act is really two events, an inner event of making the decision to kick the dog and a publicly observable physical event. In the case of the disability, the inner event is missing. Let's call this account of intentional action the two-event theory.

The two-event theory has an unfortunate consequence. It leads to the conclusion that one can never tell whether another person is acting intentionally or is simply acting under hypnosis or some disorder that mimics intentional action. This conclusion follows because what distinguishes intentional action from, for example, the behavior of a sophisticated robot is a private nonobservable event. Suppose I try to find out whether Johnson kicked the dog intentionally by asking him, and suppose he answers affirmatively. His response may be an action that he, as a robot or as a person suffering from an odd disorder, is programmed to give. Thus, my question gets me no further in finding out whether his act is intentional. In fact, no test that I can make will get me any further because each piece of evidence in turn may be impeached as an outer event unaccompanied by an inner event.

This theory has other unsatisfactory consequences. It

[12] See pages 183–196.

refers to inner events but these events are elusive. I can say that *I* used the example of Johnson and the dachshund intentionally, I can identify the "outer" event of writing about the example, but I cannot say—however much I try to do the introspection—just when the inner event occurred. I intentionally had breakfast this morning, but I cannot identify an inner event of "intending to have breakfast." Rather, there was just the single event, having breakfast, an event that I was aware of carrying out. Thus, if the theory is supposed to tell me how *I* can tell whether my own acts are intentional, it fails. I readily know when my acts are intentional, but I do not come to know this by identifying an inner event.

Still other problems are that the theory tells us nothing about how the inner and outer events are connected to each other. We know, for example, something about the connection between a pin prick and the "inner" experience of pain. Each can be identified and described separately, and each may occur without the other. But I do not know how to identify my intention to have breakfast as an event in time that is separable and separately describable from my having breakfast. The entire question about the nature of the connection seems wrongly put, but it is a natural consequence of the two-event theory.[13]

Let's review how we reached this predicament. We began by asking what distinguishes an intended act from a mere physical occurrence. The two-event theory seemed an appropriate answer. But it is an answer that tells us that the concrete question about another person, "Did he intend his actions?," can never be answered. More-

[13] Still another problem with the two-event theory is that it gives no account of why one feels that an intended action is felt to be *my own* action whereas an unintended action (or piece of behavior) is not. In other words, what is it about the so-called inner event that makes an act "mine"?

over, it does not explain our own introspective awareness of intention but seems to estrange us from what we
seem to know about ourselves.

Several distinctions will help us to see why the two-
event theory is misconceived and to come up with a
more acceptable account. Obviously, it is human nature
that I can only have my own feelings, thoughts, and
intentions. *If* the criterion for knowing someone's
thoughts, is to have them, then indeed I cannot know
another's thoughts. But we shall see that the criterion
may be a different one. Second, *if* a requirement of
knowing someone's thoughts is to be able to eliminate
any *logical* possibility that they are feigning or pretend-
ing when they tell us about their thoughts or give other
evidence, then again it is impossible to satisfy this
requirement. But it is usually sufficient to eliminate
any *practical* doubt and leave the logical possibility of
pretense aside. Finally, it is one thing to say that we
have only secondary evidence of another person's
thoughts and feelings because such matters are inevitably private. It is something else to say this about intentions because, as I shall now try to show, intentions are
not private in the ways thoughts and feelings are.

To see why intentions are not private events, consider
these facts. If I say I just thought about Halloween and
felt happy, it is appropriate for me to be asked *when* I
had the thought or feeling or how long the feeling
lasted. If I say I intentionally had breakfast at home,
it is often not meaningful to ask when I had the intention. Moreover, when I have a thought or feeling, I am
not thereby committed to any action; I may suffer a
pain in silence, stoically. If, on the other hand, I intend
to give an examination and take no action to carry out
that intention, my position is unintelligible. Someone
may say correctly, as a matter of logic, that to have an
intention *is* to be disposed to carry out the action. Of
course, circumstances may prevent me from realizing

my intention or may lead me to change my mind. But
an intention is at least a commitment to act *or* to give
a reason why one has been deflected from acting; otherwise, one simply does not have the relevant intention.

What is the importance of this? It suggests, I think,
that intending is not an inner event that precedes or
accompanies an outer event, but that it is a way in
which action alone, a single event, may be characterized and qualified. If Jones robs a bank at the point of
a gun, if Smith robs it under hypnosis, and if Anderson
does it to pay for a Rolls-Royce, I will say that only
Anderson acted intentionally. Nonetheless, each carried
out a single act. Both Jones and Anderson were conscious of what they were doing; they were conscious of
different circumstances, the one of being constrained,
the other of pursuing goals. But "intending" does not
refer to the contents of consciousness, as the case of
absent-mindedly having-and-intending-to-have breakfast
shows. Both Smith and Anderson engaged in preparatory actions or were subject to preparatory events;
Smith was placed under hypnosis and Anderson found
a getaway car. But again "intending" does not refer
to other events or actions. Rather, it tells us what the
action in question is *not:* an intentional action is not
done under constraint or coercion, not done under
hypnosis or while sleep-walking, and so on. To say it is
intentional is to say it is an example of the normal sort
of goal-oriented activity that persons engage in most of
the time when special circumstances like those listed
do not intrude and take actions out of their hands. It
may be goal oriented and yet be entirely routine and
unreflective, like brushing one's teeth.

To say that action is intentional or voluntary is, therefore, not to say that something special, an inner event,
has occurred, but to say that nothing special, no special
constraint or special cause, has occurred, none (that is)
of the special reasons we have for withdrawing the

ordinary assumption that persons are responsible for what they do. When it comes to determining whether these special reasons apply to a case, there are ways of finding and using evidence. Did Walker act at the point of a gun? Was Hanson suffering from paranoid delusions? Was Benson drugged? These are questions that we know how to go about answering and they are the sorts of questions that, if answered negatively, will yield the conclusion that Walker, Hanson, and Benson acted intentionally, freely, and are to be held responsible. There is no need to look for an inner event.

We can summarize these observations. We have seen that the term *intentionally* adverbially modifies action and does not refer to an inner event. Rather it refers to the ordinary mode of action in which persons pursue goals without coercion, constraint, or lapse of consciousness.[14] An unrealized intention is not an inner event lacking an outer correlative event; it is a kind of disposition to behave in a certain way. Although there are inner experiences that may accompany actions— the silent making of a resolution, a fantasized anticipation of one's actions, or planning activity—none of the inner experiences is designated by the term *intention* or is a necessary aspect of intentional activity.

The fact that we are able to make judgments about the intentions of others is a fact about human experience that makes possible criminal law as we know it. Having seen why it is possible and having examined the kinds of evidence relevant to such judgments, I shall turn later in this chapter to some of specific ways in which the law uses that evidence.[15]

---

[14] The notion of constraint is ambiguous. There is a sense in which one acts intentionally even when one acts under severe constraint. Handing over my wallet to a gunman, I nonetheless intend to satisfy the demand and protect myself from harm.

[15] I am not assuming that *voluntary, intentional,* and *free* are synonyms. There are important differences among these terms but these differences are not particularly relevant to this discussion.

Moral and Legal Responsibility

At the beginning of Chapter 3 we considered several reasons why law is not and cannot be "the enforcement of morals."[16] In this section, I shall look at additional reasons why the criteria for legal liability (or legal responsibility)[17] diverge from those for moral responsibility. Our main concern here will be the criteria found in criminal law.

Before looking once more at moral responsibility, let us sketch the outlines of the concept of legal liability and of the picture of human nature that underlies that concept. As we have seen, legal liability (and moral responsibility as well) presupposes that persons have control over their actions, that they have the capacity to act voluntarily and exercise free choice. Accordingly, in modern criminal codes the criteria for liability are characterized by the Latin terms, *mens rea* (guilty mind) and *actus reus* (guilty act). The requirement that there be an *actus reus* is satisfied when the offense of which a person is accused was in fact committed, when the person charged in fact performed the relevant act and did so voluntarily. These requirements are illustrated by the following examples. Someone who attempts to kill his rival and shoots but misses, or someone who hits his rival but fails to kill him because the victim is wearing a bulletproof vest cannot be held for murder. He can, however, be held for attempted murder, for which the penalties are usually lower. These requirements mean that the person charged must be *proved* to have carried out the act and that he must have carried it out while he had the capacity to act in general. In other

---

[16] See Chapter 3, pages 121–127.

[17] I am choosing to treat "legal responsibility" and "legal liability" as referring to the same notion. Various relationships among these notions are discussed very well by H. L. A. Hart in *Punishment and Responsibility* (Oxford, 1968), Chapter IX.

words, the requirement of an *actus reus* is not satisfied if the act was committed under hypnosis, while sleepwalking, and so on. This last aspect is usually called the requirement of voluntariness, but this is misleading. It does not mean that the actor necessarily chose to act as he did or that the actions were willed. Rather, it merely excludes the possibility that the person's bodily motions were in the power of some outside agent, like a hypnotist, or in the control of some automatism, like a reflex or sleepwalking. Someone who takes a life while driving negligently is, by this standard, acting voluntarily.

The requirement that there be a *mens rea* is the requirement that the act be done in a state of mind appropriate to liability. This does not mean that the actor must know that he or she is disobeying the law. One is liable for larceny or assault even if one is ignorant of the fact that they are forbidden. It does mean, however, that the actor must either have intended to do harm or have acted knowingly or recklessly with the awareness that he or she was doing harm.[18] At a minimum, we must be able to say with confidence that a reasonable person in that position would have been aware that he or she was doing harm. The theory behind the *mens rea* requirement is that, while we extend punishment beyond the class of those who intend harm, we must be satisfied that those who are held liable and punished had a fair opportunity to conform their behavior to what is required by law.[19] Many theorists find it helpful to clarify the *mens rea* requirement by indicating how it is *not* satisfied, by listing conditions that excuse a person from liability or that justify such acts. Examples are harmful acts committed under duress or the threats of others, acts done under the mistaken apprehension

[18] I am following the Model Penal Code's categories and distinctions in discussing *mens rea* and the levels of culpability.
[19] See Hart, op. cit., Chapter VII.

that one's acts were not harmful, acts committed while insane, and harm caused in self-defense.[20]

There are exceptions to this very general analysis. Not everything that the law forbids is, on its face, a harm-causing act. Certain practices may be regulated by use of criminal penalties when there is merely a potential for harm or when special care is needed to prevent harm. One may violate laws concerning the preparation of food or drugs or concerning the issuing of securities even though the particular violation does not involve harm. It is customary to refer to such crimes as *malum prohibitum* (bad as prohibited) rather than *malum in se* (bad in itself). In some prosecutions for crimes that are *malum prohibitum* the *mens rea* requirement is dispensed with because of the overriding importance of regulation or because *mens rea* is unusually difficult to establish.

There are also qualifications as well as exceptions. The requirement of *actus reus* can be satisfied in some situations in which no harm is realized (the law of attempts) or in which the offender is not the primary agent of harm (the law of conspiracy; accomplice liability). The requirement of *mens rea* may be satisfied even when it is established that the offender had no real opportunity to avoid the harm-causing acts because, for example, he was much more ignorant than the ordinary person. The offender who believes truly but unreasonably that he is wielding a toy rather than a gun may be held liable for his actions.

The study of criminal law is largely the study of how these requirements have been interpreted for specific

---

[20]There is an important distinction between excuses and justifications. An act that would otherwise be criminal is excusable to the extent that facts establish the absence of *mens rea.* Examples are cases of duress and cases of excusable mistake. An act is justifiable on the other hand when it is done intentionally but the actor is privileged. Examples are the taking of a life in self-defense or by an officer empowered to prevent felonies.

crimes and various situations.[21] Why has criminal law taken this shape? I am concerned not with historical or sociological answers but with the philosophical question of justification. What reasons can be given for having a criminal law with this general shape rather than some other?

The form of a utilitarian justification would be that *this* set of rules rather than another set of rules works best to maximize benefit; it works to secure those benefits about which there is a consensus in the society and to achieve acceptable compromises with regard to those values that are controversial. It is noteworthy that the framework I have sketched prevails in most modern societies. There is general agreement that sanctions[22] should be applied only to actual harm-doers and only when they have acted in a culpable state of mind. (Obviously, the practice within a society may diverge from the principles embodied in the structure of criminal law. The abuse of criminal law to suppress political dissent is a common example. When abuse occurs, it is characteristically camouflaged by attempts to show that political prisoners are culpable by objective [non-political] criteria.)

The observation that most systems of criminal law share this structure is so familiar that we tend to over-look its significance. We forget that there are other possibilities that our society and others have rejected. For example, one might have a system in which the government randomly punished persons, selected by lot, at a rate proportional to the crime rate. Such a system would be cheap and efficient since there would

[21] Two recent books that discuss the theory of criminal law in detail are Hyman Gross, *A Theory of Criminal Justice* (Oxford, 1979), and George Fletcher, *Rethinking Criminal Law* (Boston, 1978).

[22] I shall be using the word *sanctions* in place of *punishments* at certain points because sanctions may be applied either to the innocent and the guilty, whereas punishing the innocent seems in one sense to be a self-contradictory notion.

be no investigation or adjudication. It would give everyone an incentive to keep others from committing crimes, because that would minimize the risk of sanctions for all. And it would spread some of the costs of deterrence in a procedurally equitable way. Why then is such a system unacceptable? The reason, I assume, is that the costs obviously outweigh the benefits. The lives of all would be made insecure, because all would be potential victims of governmental sanctions. Moreover, such a system would be unlikely to deter potential criminals effectively; the risk that they would be picked for sanctions would be low unless sanctions were widely distributed. Thus, a system that generally did away with the requirement of an *actus reus* for liability would be unlikely to diminish crime and would introduce its own special kinds of harm. When we say that such a system would be unfair or unjust,[23] we express our intuitions about relative harm; we express the sense that general well-being in this kind of hypothetical society would be lessened in an unacceptable way.

Our response to this hypothetical situation reflects the importance of the *mens rea* requirement as well as the *actus reus* requirement. The unacceptable harm here has two components, the fear and insecurity that each member of such a society will naturally suffer and the actual harm inflicted on those who are picked for sanctions. The conviction is that neither kind of harm should be inflicted on those who do not deserve it; the subclass of harm-doers who deserve sanctions are those who were in a position to avoid doing harm and nevertheless went forward. The harm is equally unjustifiable whether it is inflicted on scapegoats who did no harm or on those who did harm unwittingly or involuntarily. The underlying rationale is that to impose

[23] The relationship of fairness and justice is explored by John Rawls in *A Theory of Justice* (Cambridge, 1971).

sanctions more widely is to harm everyone's well-being by increasing their risk of being harmed regardless of whether they did harm at all or did so avoidably. (This last point is controversial. Some theorists have argued that more is to be gained than lost by extending liability to those who cause harm but lack *mens rea*. I shall consider such suggestions in pages 121–126.)

This account of the general justification of criminal law must be qualified in the following ways.

(1) All societies recognize that there are special circumstances of an urgent and temporary nature in which it is justifiable to suspend these limits on liability. If terrorism or guerrila warfare is widespread, a government may be justified in suspending the *mens rea* requirement and holding liable all persons found to possess dangerous weapons or ingredients for making bombs. In still more exigent circumstances, all members of a political party may be detained and sanctioned if their leaders have declared war on the community as a whole. In this way the requirement of an *actus reus* may be suspended. This raises the difficult question of how serious the threat must be before officials are morally entitled to apply sanctions to surrogates who are in effect scapegoats and to do so for purposes of deterrence.

(2) We have just seen that a government may justifiably suspend some of the limits of liability to meet an exigent situation. It is also the case that an individual may justifiably invade these limits if he or she is under unusual constraint. A response that could not be translated into a justifiable general rule may be justifiable as a particular response to an emergency.

Suppose the hijackers of a plane threaten to blow it up in flight unless a political refugee is returned by the United States to Cuba, where he faces almost certain death. To return the refugee and yield to the hijackers' demands would be to treat the refugee as a scapegoat. But the rule against scapegoating may not

be decisive when the costs of following the rule may
be the loss of many innocent lives. There is an irreducible difference between setting a general policy and
applying it in particular cases. The policy and the
violation of that policy in special cases may both be
justifiable.

(3) In describing the general limits of liability, the
general framework of a justifiable criminal law, I am
not speaking for all societies and all times. Anthro-
pologists tell us about societies in which the punishing
of scapegoats, of a representative member of the harm-
doer's family, for example, was common practice.[24]
In Nazi Germany, Jews were expropriated and killed
not on the basis of individual culpability but on the
basis of heritage and affiliation.

In sorting out such examples we need to distinguish
societies that have no recognizable standards corres-
ponding to *mens rea* and *actus reus* from societies that
apply such criteria in ways very different from our
own. The content of *mens rea* is filled in by factual
knowledge about human psychology. Such knowledge
changes and evolves over time. The diverse forms that
the insanity defense has taken in our history and in
different Western societies are a good example of this.

We must also distinguish societies that are influenced
by the liberal and humanistic notion of the dignity
of each individual and of his or her right to self-
development. The model of criminal law that we are
describing is appropriate for, and likely to arise in,
such societies.

Most of the interesting controversies within criminal
law are about how the general structure we have been
describing is to be translated into rules and procedures.

---

[24] See "Scapegoat," *Encyclopedia Britannica,* Micropaedia, 8, 945
(Chicago, 1978).

It is one thing to say that a justifiable system will determine individual culpability by recourse to criteria of *mens rea* and *actus reus*. It is something else to agree on what interpretation of these criteria will best achieve the purposes of law by maximizing well-being (or benefit) in society. Consider the following issues.

(1) We have already seen that many kinds of strict liability offenses (*malum prohibitum*) have been created in the last twenty to thirty years. Such statutes are justified, it is said, because certain activities present so serious a potential danger to public welfare that persons engaged in them can be assumed to be on notice that they have a special duty of care. Examples are the production and sale of drugs, the manufacture and sale of explosives, and the processing of food. Also, it is said to be so easy to conceal negligence in such cases that an inquiry is not likely to yield evidence of faulty behavior. Accordingly, strict liability cases are described as ones in which *mens rea* is not an element of the offense and in which liability attaches automatically on proof of *actus reus*. At the same time, severe penalties cannot be inflicted for strict liability offenses, because this would violate a general sense of what is a justifiable exception to the general limits of liability.[25]

The theory and limits of strict liability are less clear than they appear. Does the theory presuppose that in these cases a culpable state of mind, a failure to take sufficient care, is present but unprovable? Or is the theory that even a conclusory determination of failure of care is *irrelevant?* Either theory would justify strict liability offenses but with different results. Suppose a certain chemical were such that it exploded without warning under very rare and unpredictable atmospheric

[25] In constitutional law the notion of "substantive due process" is often used to describe such constitutional limits on liability. To go beyond these limits is to violate each person's constitutional right to be treated with due process.

conditions. By the first theory, a processor or transporter would not be liable for an explosion because there could be no presumption of negligence. By the second theory, he would still be liable. The question, in other words, is whether strict liability offenses are a modification of or an exception to the *mens rea* requirement.

Other controversial aspects of strict liability offenses are these. Is imprisonment ever an appropriate sanction for such an offense, or ought sanctions to be limited to fines, adverse publicity, and so on? If sanctions are limited to fines, is criminal law the appropriate forum for such litigation or are there good reasons for transferring these cases to civil law?[26]

(2) A related controversy is the extension of the doctrine of *respondeat superior* to corporate crime. This is the doctrine, familiar in tort (accident) law, that holds that a person may be held liable in appropriate circumstances for the acts of an agent, employee, or child. Extension of this doctrine to criminal law flies in the face of individualized liability. At the same time, some of the same arguments that support strict liability offenses also support extension of *respondeat superior*. The criminal acts of an employee (for example, the theft of the research plans of a competitor) may benefit the employer and may seem to be instigated by the employer. But evidence of the employer's complicity may be hard to find and easy to conceal. Thus, some theorists have endorsed a conclusive presumption that an employer is liable whenever he has placed the em-

---

[26] This is an important difference. Criminal and civil cases are conducted differently and the rights of defendants in the two sorts of cases vary. A criminal has to be proven guilty beyond a reasonable doubt; a civil case is won when it is established by a preponderance of the evidence that one party or the other has the right to a favorable verdict. It is debated whether the constitutional safeguards imposed on criminal litigation are appropriate to strict liability cases that involve minor penalties and no consideration of *mens rea.*

ployee in a position to carry out the illegal activity and
when the criminal activity primarily benefits the employer. It is argued by opponents of this suggestion
that employers (officers of the company, the board
of a corporation) should be liable only if they have
ratified or overseen the acts of the employee.

(3) Another debate about the limits and justification
of the *mens rea* requirement is the debate over felony
murder. The issue takes the following form. Murder and
manslaughter are two degrees of unjustifiable homicide.
Murder, which is punished more severely, is the intentional taking of a life, or the taking of it while fore-
seeing the result of one's actions; manslaughter is a
reckless or negligent taking of a life, or a taking of a
life while deranged by sudden emotion.[27] It is said,
formally, that the *actus reus* for both crimes is the
same and that they differ in *mens rea*. The felony-
murder doctrine is an exception to this distinction. It
says that one may be held for murder and not manslaughter if one accidentally causes a death in the course
of committing a dangerous and serious crime (felony).
Robbery, rape, and arson are examples. The supposed
justification of the doctrine is that it will deter felons
from committing crimes in ways that are particularly
dangerous to the lives of others.

The felony-murder doctrine is a survival from common law and is much criticized by modern writers.[28]
It is said that there can be no justification for punishing
Jones more severely than Harris when each happened
to burn down a building but Jones was unlucky enough
to cause the death of a nightwatchman inside the

---

[27] For materials explicating the murder/manslaughter distinction, see
Sanford Kadish and Monrad Paulsen (eds.), *Criminal Law and Its Processes,*
3rd ed. (Boston, 1975), Chapter 3.

[28] For the case against felony murder see Model Penal Code, Tentative
Draft No. 9 (1959), comments to ¶ 201.2 (1) (b), pp. 37–39, quoted in
Kadish and Paulsen, op. cit., pp. 280–281.

building. It is also said that the deterrence argument is unconvincing because it is impossible to carry out a dangerous felony with greater or less care. Moreover, these writers claim, the possibility of incurring a penalty for murder is unlikely to affect the behavior of those who are already bent on carrying out a dangerous crime.

(4) A more general issue that raises similar controversies is the legal treatment of attempts to commit crimes. An attempt occurs when one carries out acts that one expects, with good reason, will result in particular harm but that fail to do so because of an accidental intervention or condition. The actor shoots, but the victim ducks. Or he stabs the recumbent figure in the dark and it turns out to be a pillow, not the intended victim. A technical question is whether in such cases there is any *actus reus,* any guilty act. The answer is that the act is the series of actions carried out to further the criminal purpose. A more difficult question is whether those who are guilty of attempts ought to be punished with the same severity as those who both attempt and succeed. If failure or success is a matter of accident, it ought to be irrelevant to the penalty, it is said. Some modern statutes accept this reasoning and impose the same penalty for an attempt as for the completed crime.

The issue is a bit more complicated. These modern statutes depart from a long tradition of punishing attempts less severely. Why has this distinction existed? We have already seen that it is inherent in the requirement of *actus reus* that persons are not punishable for their wishes, fantasies, or intentions until they are on the way to carrying them out. The assumption is that to allow greater intervention in the lives of persons, as a general matter, would be to compromise the privacy and well-being of all. This is expressed in the homely phrase, "A dog is entitled to his first bite." Punishment for attempts seems to violate this principle: the dog is punished even though it has not bitten. Older, more traditional law is therefore a compromise with this principle: the penalty is lowered. The modern view is that there is no reason for compromise. To punish for attempts in this view is not at all to punish for wishes, fantasies, or intentions but for acts fully carried out.[29]

(5) The most visible area of controversy in criminal law is criminal procedure. Here we are concerned not simply with the substantive limits of liability but with the rules that control how liability is assessed in particular cases. The evolution of the law of criminal procedure can be traced largely through Supreme Court decisions interpreting the provisions of the Bill of Rights, provisions that set limits on what the government can do in investigating and prosecuting crimes.

In his influential book, *The Limits of the Criminal Sanction*,[30] Herbert Packer says that judges seem to adopt one of two theoretical positions when asked to decide what optimal balance of interests is prescribed by the Bill of Rights. The first position, which Packer calls the "crime-control" model,[31] takes it as the goal of criminal procedure to streamline the apprehension and processing of offenders so that crime is deterred through efficient enforcement. The second model, the "due-process" model,[32] places special emphasis on the need to control governmental interference in persons' lives. It says that abuse is especially frequent in the enforcement of criminal law. Thus, it stresses the need for clear and narrow guidelines regulating the use of confessions, the conduct of searches and arrests, the availability of lawyers to persons accused of crimes, and the protection of persons against self-incrimination.

---

[29] One way in which this is expressed in rules defining liability for attempts is that an attempt is complete only when the offender's actions carry him beyond the *locus penitentiae,* the point of repentance and withdrawal.

[30] (Stanford, 1968).

[31] Ibid., pp. 153–173.

[32] Ibid., pp. 153–158, 163–173.

It argues that it may be necessary to enforce these limits by letting guilty persons go, and it supports this view by saying that there are aspects of well-being in society (the enjoyment of liberty, privacy, self-determination) that may override the minimization of crime. The disagreement between the two kinds of theorists works on two levels at once. In part, it is a disagreement about such facts as the frequency of police and prosecutorial abuse or the effect on deterrence of restraining aggressive enforcement. But it is also a disagreement about what kind of society is most worth having, disagreement about what are the most important exercises of liberty.

These issues are samples of the kinds of controversies that proliferate in theoretical writings on criminal law. I have listed them and described them here to illustrate the complex relationship between legal liability and moral responsibility. That relationship can now be described as follows. On the widest level, criminal law as we know it in modern liberal[33] countries rests on a moral consensus that can be expressed in three propositions. (1) It is sometimes morally justifiable to inflict harm on persons through the power of the state to secure a general benefit or prevent a greater harm. (2) Such interventions are justifiable only when they are inflicted on persons who themselves have caused harm. (3) Such interventions are justifiable only when the offenders have had a fair opportunity to forego their harm-causing actions. In this way, the engine of criminal law is fueled by a moral purpose, the purpose of achieving those benefits that can only be achieved by implementing these principles.

On a second level, legislators and judges must decide how these principles are best implemented. In reaching

---

[33] I am using "liberal" in a very general way to refer to cultures and systems of thought influenced by such values as respect for the self-development of each person and for freedom. The roots of many of these values are in Renaissance humanism.

such decisions, they are likely to disagree among themselves in three ways. First, they may disagree about
facts, such facts as the incidence of police abuse, the
motivations of persons who fail in attempts to commit
crimes, or the incidence of corporate malfeasance. Second, they may disagree about what effect on criminal
enforcement an exclusionary rule[34] may have, or
whether a strict liability rule will have significantly
greater deterrent effect than one that takes *mens rea*
into account. Third, they may disagree about what
states of affairs are more desirable, more beneficial overall, than others. Even if they are in agreement about
all relevant facts and predictions, they may disagree
about such matters as whether it is good to let a guilty
person go free for the sake of vindicating a principle
like the prohibition against self-incrimination. Or they
may disagree about whether it is good to compel employers to scrutinize the behavior of their employees
for the appearance of criminal conduct.

Of these kinds of disagreement, only the third seems
to be a moral disagreement, a disagreement in their
conceptions of benefit and harm. But, in another sense,
all three kinds are disagreements about how persons
in society are most benefited and least harmed. Disagreements in fact or prediction are disagreements about
facts and predictions that are to be used in assessing
benefit and harm. From this point of view, all three
kinds of disagreement are moral disagreements; more
precisely, all three are disagreements about the nature
and consequences of legal acts that have moral effects.

We can draw some conclusions. The first is that even
though not all legal disputes are moral disputes, they
are all disputes in which moral effects (benefit and
harm) are at stake. Second, moral agreement alone
cannot resolve legal disputes because special legal ques-

[34]The exclusionary rule is the rule that evidence acquired through a
violation of the defendant's rights cannot be used at trial against him
however reliable that evidence may be.

tions must also be settled, questions about, for example, the probable effect of changed laws on attitudes and behavior. And the third point is that such disputes may well be unending.

The Justification of Punishment

We saw that criminal law presents special problems of justification because here the state takes it upon itself to inflict harm on persons (as punishment). Although there are other areas of law in which the state directly inflicts harm—taxation is one example, the military draft is another—the burden in these other areas is spread as widely and fairly as possible for a purpose that, it is argued, is equally in the interest of all who are burdened. Criminal punishment is altogether different. A particular individual is singled out for special harm and he or she is *not* arguably the ultimate beneficiary.

The most obvious purpose of punishment is restraint (special deterrence). That is, punishment keeps the offender from doing more harm both by incapacitating him, putting him in jail for example, and by teaching the lesson that new crimes will be likely to lead to similar punishments. A second purpose is general deterrence. Punishing the offender is a warning and an example to others who may be tempted to commit such crimes. Finally, it is said, there is the purpose of rehabilitation. Incarceration gives the state an opportunity to help the offender lead a better life.

Not all of these purposes will be served in every case. The person who kills from provocation and in sudden anger may not need restraint or rehabilitation, but the punishment may serve general deterrence.[35] Also, some

---

[35] General deterrence may be served by punishing some persons who have not chosen or intended to commit crimes insofar as it may induce persons to take special precautions to avoid situations in which they run a risk of killing out of provocation, for example.

of these purposes are more elusive than others. Restraint is easy; rehabilitation is difficult both because we are unable or unwilling (politically) to give over the needed resources and because we don't know how to rehabilitate.[36] For example, we don't know how to overcome the psychological damage of early social deprivation and extreme poverty.

These purposes are all forward looking. They are all parts of a utilitarian justification for punishment that says that a greater good is achieved through inflicting the harm of punishment. As such, they have inspired some writers to ask whether the same purposes would not justify other systems, some of which may involve scapegoats. Suppose we found we could deter murder and rape by punishing all persons suspected of these crimes without a judicial determination of guilt. Would this practice also be justified by utilitarian argument? The suggestion is that utilitarianism justifies too much; the same purposes would be achieved by unacceptable practices.

This criticism is often part of a larger argument. It is said that retribution, not forward-looking goals, is the basis of criminal law. We punish persons because they are blameworthy and their blameworthiness is both the cause and the justification for doing so. Moreover, the degree of punishment should be measured by the degree of blame. In this way, retributivists account for the limitation of punishment to actual offenders and not scapegoats. The theory is "backward looking" because it looks at features of the offender and the offense in determining punishment and not at purposes to be achieved.

[36]Of the three purposes, general deterrence is less controversial than rehabilitation. It is clear as a general matter that punishing an act and publicizing the fact that it will be punished will dissuade some persons from so acting. At the same time, some kinds of crimes (economic crimes, for example) are more easily deterred than others (crimes of passion). And it is hard to "fine-tune" a deterrent because many factors will affect the incidence of crime and the specific effects of particular penalties are hard to isolate.

One difficulty with retributivism is that blameworthiness seems to have no objective measure. *Feelings* of blame are compounded of anger, resentment, and fear, and such feelings are notoriously variable and unpredictable. They vary from person to person, and they vary in a given person with that individual's experiences, capacity for sympathy, knowledge of human suffering and frailty, and relation to the particular case. As we saw in Chapter 3,[37] feelings alone do not count as moral justification. In themselves, anger and resentment do not justify political or legal action any more than envy and lust. There are many reasons why persons have the feelings they have and only some of those reasons have relevance in moral justification.

We can salvage the retributivist's argument only by separating blameworthiness from feelings of blame. One must look instead for objective measures of blameworthiness. One such measure may be the kind and amount of harm caused by the offender. Another measure would be his attitudes and expectations toward his actions, in particular his intentions. These are all factors, the retributivist tells us, in determining whether the offender *deserves* punishment, and punishment ought to be proportional to desert.

We have now arrived, from a retributivist rather than a utilitarian standpoint, at an account of the importance of *actus reus* and *mens rea*. But it is important to see what this account does *not* tell us. It answers the questions who to punish and how much to punish; it does not answer the question why punish. The theory assumes rather than explains why blameworthiness justifies punishment. How can this question be answered?

The question of why blameworthiness justifies punishment is really the same question as whether utilitarian

---

[37]See Ronald Dworkin, *Taking Rights Seriously* (Cambridge, 1978), Chapter 10; these matters were discussed at length in Chapter 3.

and retributive theories are compatible. Let me explain. It is not by accident that the most blameworthy person is also the person most in need of restraint and re-habilitation, and that the most blameworthy classes of action are those we most need to deter. The most blameworthy person tends to be the most dangerous person as well. It is not true, therefore, that judgments of blameworthiness are backward looking; they have anticipatory aspects as well.

The process of punishing the blameworthy has second-ary effects that are also forward looking. The visible process of trial and conviction is an affirmation of the values that hold society together.[38] A society in which standards are stable and visible is one in which the quality of life is improved for all. A system of rules in which persons who are not blameworthy are punished has adverse secondary effects. Persons are less secure; the most respectable ways of living, from a moral stand-point, are not given recognition and morally excusable behavior is not pardoned and forgiven.

Of course, there is no societal benefit in shared stan-dards *per se*. A community may be bound by standards that curtail freedom, restrain personal development, or oppress a minority. Such standards harm those who are subject to them and corrupt those who enforce them. Well-being is fostered by shared standards only when they enforce an uncontroversial minimal standard of harm and blameworthiness and when they otherwise support mutual respect and the exercise of liberty for self-development.

We can now see clearly the relationship between utilitarianism and retributivism and the place of the notions of desert and blameworthiness in a utilitarian account. From a utilitarian standpoint, there are com-pelling reasons to limit punishment to those who are

---

[38] See Hart, *Punishment and Responsibility,* Chapter IX.

blameworthy. This achieves the forward-looking goal of restraining those who are most dangerous while knitting society together by reinforcing the underlying values involved in having mutual respect. Even if we could achieve some forward-looking goals, general deterrence, for example, by casting the net more broadly, the secondary costs are likely to be too great. Security and mutual respect of persons for each other and for their government would be compromised too severely. It follows that blameworthiness or desert is a threshold for eligibility to be punished. The utilitarian has forward-looking reasons for maintaining it as a threshold. In this way, the utilitarian can incorporate the remarks of the retributivist and meet his criticisms.

So far, I have addressed the question who to punish and I have shown that utilitarian answers can accommodate the notions of blame and desert. But the questions *how much* to punish reintroduces tension between utilitarianism and retributivism. Consider the example of a legislator who takes bribes to vote for pieces of legislation. Public exposure seems to be an adequate sanction because restraint and general deterrence are likely to be served. However, a theory of desert would seem to demand more because an offender who violates a public trust is particularly blameworthy. On the other hand, consider the case of a thief who steals because his family is poor and hungry. He is not particularly blameworthy. Nonetheless, the law looks to the goal of general deterrence and restraint and disallows poverty as a justification or mitigating condition. The penalty may be quite severe.

These tensions have the following partial explanation. Blameworthiness and desert are individualized notions that are to be applied case-by-case. In law there is need for visible prohibitions that are uniformly applied. Thus it is both undesirable and impracticable to create a system of enforcement that is sensitive to the limitless personal factors that affect a moral determination of blameworthiness. Rules would be dissolved into a welter of exceptions. A sense of blameworthiness does, however, have two roles to play. It supplies intuitions about what general categories of crimes are to be punished more severely than others because they involve greater harm or greater malice. And it supplies considerations that may be irrelevant to a finding of guilt or innocence but altogether relevant to the question of individualized sentencing.

Insanity and the Elimination of Responsibility

Any discussion of the justification of punishment must take account of two special cases, the insane offender and the so-called moral criminal. In this section, I shall consider the first of these.

The insane harm-doer presents a special problem because he lacks one of the conditions of liability, the capacity for responsibility. We have seen that persons may be liable for intentional acts, reckless acts, and negligent acts with very serious consequences. In all these situations the actor has a general capacity for responsibility. He is capable of acting on intentions and restraining himself from doing harm. In general this cannot be said of the insane offender.

Does this mean that the insane person cannot satisfy the requirement of *mens rea?*[39] Not necessarily. Imagine that Anderson has the paranoical delusion that Johnson is stealing from him and harrassing him. He sets out to kill Johnson and makes careful plans, which he carries out over a period of several weeks. Anderson seems in this case to have formed an intention and to have

[39] See Jay Katz and Joseph Goldstein, "Abolish the Insanity Defense—Why Not?," *Yale Law Journal,* 72, 853 (1963).

carried it out. He seems, that is, to satisfy the conditions of *mens rea*. The special importance of insanity is that the machinery whereby the intentions are formed and carried out is diseased and disturbed. Anderson is out of touch with reality and unable to fit his plans and actions to a reasonable life plan, whether it is criminal or not.[40]

Accordingly, criminal law does not allow proof of insanity under *mens rea* but creates a special insanity defense. Formally, a person who satisfies the conditions of criminal liability will be acquitted if he or she also satisfies the conditions set by the insanity defense. Over the years, American courts have had much difficulty in setting a test for juries to use in determining whether defendants are insane.[41] There are many reasons for this. The nature of insanity is both complex and controversial. Although it is easy to find examples of severe disturbance and examples of normal human functioning, it is not at all clear that there is a continuum between the two or that there is a point on such a continuum that separates the sane from the insane. Most persons suffer from some neurotic behavior patterns, some obsessions, repressed wishes, and so on. It is not at all clear how severe a disturbance must be to qualify as insanity. And it is sometimes said that the committing of a crime is itself the best possible evidence of severe disturbance.[42] Other difficulties with the insanity defense are institutional. Jury mem-

[40] See Joel Feinberg, *Doing and Deserving* (Princeton, 1970), Chapter 10, for an excellent discussion of these matters.

[41] These developments are well described and analyzed in Abraham Goldstein, *The Insanity Defense* (New Haven, 1967).

[42] A sociopath carries out antisocial actions; sociopathy is not a psychological designation and says nothing about character or motivational structure. A psychopath is someone who lacks the normal restraints of empathy and sympathy for harm and suffering; psychopathy is a clinical diagnostic term. Sociopaths in general are not insane, given standard legal definitions; psychopathy, on the other hand, is often regarded as a form of insanity.

bers are often unsophisticated and need to be instructed by experts in psychology. At the same time, experts often have conflicting paradigms of insanity and are themselves not equipped to find a mythical line between insanity and sanity.

The result of an acquittal for insanity is usually not the freeing of the offender. He is usually committed for treatment,[43] sometimes for an indefinite period. Thus, the consequences to the offender are unlike the consequences of any other defense. In obvious ways, they are much like the consequences of conviction.

The treatment of the insane creates special problems for a theory of justification, especially for one that seeks to fit the notion of desert or blameworthiness to a utilitarian framework. On the one hand, committing the insane offender serves forward-looking goals by restraining and incapacitating him and giving some opportunity for treatment. On the other hand, we are compromising the goal of harming only those who have had a fair opportunity to comply with the law. This problem is not remedied by simply labeling the harm "treatment" rather than "punishment."

For some writers, the situation is indefensible.[44] They argue that the use of the insanity defense varies so greatly with the idiosyncracies of juries and the theoretical biases of experts that the results are entirely random. They argue, moreover, that there is no possibility of finding an improved test for insanity that will remedy the problem. And finally they argue that sane and insane offenders equally need to be restrained because both are dangerous, and therefore we need not differentiate between them.

Their solution is radical. Barbara Wootton, the best-known proponent, suggests not only that the insanity

---

[43] State codes vary in making commitment after an aquittal on grounds of insanity compulsory or discretionary.

[44] Barbara Wootton, *Crime and the Criminal Law* (London, 1963).

defense be eliminated but also that liability not be based on any assessment of *mens rea*.[45] She describes a two-step adjudication process. At the first stage, acquittal or conviction is based only on a determination of *actus reus*. The second stage is a hearing at which experts decide how those who have been convicted are to be treated to best achieve the goals of restraint, general deterrence, and rehabilitation. Only at the second stage is there an inquiry into the mind, attitudes, and capacities of the offender. Because the system makes no mention of blameworthiness or moral responsibility and has no use for such notions, Lady Wootton correctly says that her system "eliminates" responsibility. She defends this result in part by saying that the causal explainability of behavior shows that responsibility and free will are myths.[46]

Lady Wootton's proposal invites several responses. On the most general theoretical level, one can contest the assumption that responsibility is a myth. I have discussed this response at length in pages 183–196 of this chapter. One can also question in what sense blameworthiness is eliminable and whether its elimination is desirable. On the first point, it is very hard to see how one may conceive of one's own actions or those of others without using in some way the category of responsibility. This would mean that the distinctions between compelled and uncompelled actions and between voluntary and involuntary actions would drop out of our conceptual apparatus. We would not speak or think of persons as being responsible or not responsible for what they have done. Moreover we would have to be able to experience the institutional application of norms without relating that application to approval and disapproval, because these attitudes imply that

[45] Ibid.
[46] See Alf Ross's discussion of Wootton's position in *On Guilt, Responsibility and Punishment* (Berkeley, 1975), Chapter 4.

there is responsibility and blame. It is no easier to see what aspects of self-understanding or self-description would survive this purge than it is to imagine oneself a self-conscious billiard ball.[47]

Even if this were clearly conceived and imaginable, even if we could apply legal rules of conduct as if they had nothing to do with responsibility, would this be desirable? Note that such a system of law would lose its secondary function of reinforcing mutual respect for persons. Note also that the legitimacy of law and the readiness of most persons to comply with it seems to have much to do with its moral content. These purposes would be sacrificed, and for what gain?

The theoretical foundations of Wootton's proposal are obviously not well thought out. Would she eliminate responsibility from man's conception of himself altogether (as she would have to do if it were a myth)? Or would she eliminate it from the justification of law and leave our moral assumptions intact? And how could either possibility be brought about? All of these questions have no clear answer. It is possible however to put aside this theoretical muddle and consider the proposal solely as a recommendation for procedural reform.[48] Writers like H. L. A. Hart and Joel Feinberg[49] have conceded that it may be impossible to give juries a usable test for insanity and that it may be best to leave questions about the disposition of insane offenders to experts and psychological professionals rather than to juries. They have both endorsed modified forms of the two-step determination. Both would retain some inquiry into *mens rea* at the first stage; it would matter whether

[47] See Thomas Morawetz, "The Relevance of Responsibility" (a review of Ross), *Yale Law Journal*, **85**, 447 (1976).

[48] The difficulty here is that the Constitution requires that no one be convicted of a crime without due process and that due process is usually said to include a positive determination of responsibility and *mens rea.*

[49] Hart, *Punishment and Responsibility*, Chapter VII; Feinberg, *Doing and Deserving*, Chapter 10.

the offender acted intentionally or with foreknowledge, whether he acted by chance or accident, and so forth. A finding of guilt would be a *prima facie* finding of dangerousness. At the second stage, as in Wootton's model, a panel of experts (in psychology, sociology, religion, penology, and so on) would decide the disposition of the offender. At this stage evidence of sanity or insanity would be relevant. Hart and Feinberg warn, as Wootton does not, that the discretion of such a panel would have to be hedged in by procedural checks and balances designed to secure the rights of offenders. Among such rights would be uniform sentencing (insofar as it is possible), fixed and predictable terms of imprisonment (whenever feasible), and periodic review.

I shall not attempt to decide the merits of existing procedures in comparison with these hypothetical reforms. Instead I shall point out what hard questions would have to be answered before we would be in a position to make such a decision. One question is whether the project of formulating an adequate jury test for insanity can succeed. Another is whether there is any inherent value in having a determination about sanity and therefore about responsibility made by lay representatives of the community. Still a third is whether questions about the disposition of lives of offenders are the sorts of questions that ought to be or can be answered by professionals in the social sciences.

Intention, Motive, and the Moral Criminal

One difference between moral and legal judgments is that moral judgments usually take account of the actor's motive while legal judgments do not. Suppose Armstrong gives poison to his aged and ailing grandmother. It affects our moral judgment to know whether his motive is mercy or greed, whether he wants to put her out of her misery or to speed his inheritance. Criminal law looks at intention but not motive. In either hypothesis, Armstrong would be held for premeditated murder. Why is there this distinction? To be able to answer, we must first be able to distinguish between intentions and motives.

Motives are states of character or dispositions that are related to goals or ends. Ambition, the acquisition of wealth, and revenge are examples of motives. Motives may be conscious or unconscious; one may act out of jealousy and not be aware one is jealous. Even when motives are conscious, they are often not chosen: one doesn't choose to be jealous, to be ambitious, or to desire revenge. Intentions, by comparison, may be means toward ends. "Motivated by greed, he intentionally left poison for his grandmother to drink." One is usually conscious of what one intends. Indeed acting on intentions involves making choices whether or not such choices are made with much deliberation or thought.[50]

Law is concerned with intention and not motive for several reasons. Questions about motives are difficult and motives tend to be complex; there are layers to each personality and an instance of behavior may be over-determined by mixed and even contradictory motives. A conspicuous act of generosity may be motivated by the need to dominate and control the object of one's generosity. Moreover, one cannot always be held responsible for motives. They are patterns of character and action that we do not choose to have, although we may choose to develop, suppress, or modify aspects of our character that we know we have. Law, concerned with liability, is concerned with making clear judgments in areas of clear responsibility. Moral judges, on the other hand, have the luxury of making more complex and layered judgments about both the goodness of actions and intentions and about the nature of character, of virtues.

To ask juries to make guesses about motives and to

[50] See pages 196–201.

make penalties contingent on motives would be to
undercut the predictability and uniformity of justice.
It would turn jury members into amateur psychologists
and it would invite defendants to dissimulate their
motives. And it would involve punishing persons for
character traits over which they have had, in some cases,
little control.

At the same time, there are obviously situations in
which motives have to be taken into account in law.
While there are good reasons to discourage mercy-
killing and to treat the mercy-killer and the murderer
who acts out of greed equally as murderers, there are
also good reasons for mitigating the punishment in
the first case. A mercy-killing is a peripheral example
of a general class, the class of criminal acts done consciously and deliberately for a moral purpose. Examples
are acts of disobedience and protest done either because
the law requires acts that violate the actor's moral
convictions or because the effect of the law is to harm
others in a dramatic or serious way. In some such cases
the disobedient is asking the makers and appliers of law
to look again at what they have done to see whether it
works badly. The disobedient act is only a strategy for
raising this question. Here there seem to be compelling
reasons for taking motive into account.

Consider two distinctions. First, let's distinguish the
disobedient who asserts that the law is imposing an
unjustified burden on himself (by compelling military
service, for example) from the altruistic disobedient
who protests the effect of a law on others or on society
in general (by refusing to pay taxes for an illegal or
unjustified war, for example). Let's also distinguish
between the decision of such individuals (of both
kinds) to disobey and the decision of an official (prose-
cutor, judge) whether to prosecute and convict. I shall
try to show why these distinctions are important and
what tools can be used to begin to answer questions
about civil disobedience.

The disobedient who objects to an unjustified personal burden may be making one of several claims. He may say that the law imposes harm on him with no compensatory benefit to anyone else. Or that others would be benefited but that it is unjustified to single him out for special sacrifice. Both of these claims pose legislative problems. If the first claim is correct, the law is a bad law; legislators have the job of assessing law in just this way. If the second claim is correct, strategies must be used to distribute the burden as equitably as possible. The disobedient who objects for altruistic reasons may be making a stronger claim, not only that he has a right to disobey but an obligation to disobey.[51] Again the ultimate task for the legislator is to scrutinize his own determinations of relative benefit and harm to assess this claim. Disobedients of both kinds must consider not only the effects of the law that is under protest but also the exemplary effects of their disobedience in undermining respect for law. Such secondary effects may undercut or reinforce a justified decision to disobey, and this depends on whether the legal system as a whole merits reform (because it generally works more benefit than harm) or replacement (because it does not).

The question of how to treat the disobedient is separable from the question whether the disobedience is morally justified. We may approve a decision to disobey and, without inconsistency, also find justification for a decision to punish the disobedient. This will be so whenever failure to punish will seriously undermine a generally sound system of law. (In such cases there will usually be opportunities for mitigation.) This distinction is based on the general features of a utilitarian analysis of law. The justification of an action depends on its beneficial and harmful consequences.

---

[51] A useful discussion of civil disobedience and related matters is to be found in Michael Walzer, *Obligations* (Cambridge, 1970), especially Chapters 1, 2, 4, and 10.

The decision of a judge whether or not to punish has a different set of consequences from those of the disobedient's decision to disobey. It is a strength of a legal system and not a weakness—it is a kind of resilience—that it can accommodate disobedience, sensitive responses by legislators to that disobedience, and respect for the uniform enforcement of law.

Conclusions

Once again, we return to what has been a basic theme of this book, the usefulness and limits of utilitarianism as a theory of legal, political, and moral decision-making. The utilitarian takes it to be a self-evident truth that governments exist to benefit their citizens, to help all to lead better lives. Accordingly, each decision of a judge or legislator is to be evaluated by the standard of whether it contributes to the best allocation of benefits. As we have seen, it does not necessarily follow that each decision-maker should have benefit allocation directly in mind. It may be the case, as rule utilitarians claim, that optimal allocation is achieved when decision-makers follow rules that place limits on the factors that they may take into account.

So-called rights theorists mount a serious challenge to utilitarianism by putting forward a fundamentally different insight into the function of government. In their view, governments do not exist to promote and insure well-being *tout court*. Rather, they exist to preserve the independence of individuals from unwarranted interference from other individuals and from government itself. The scope of such an entitlement to protection is the scope of an individual's rights. Governments may promote well-being only to the extent that such activity does not compromise the rights of individuals.

Both theories are highly abstract and may be deployed in various ways. One's choice between the two theories may depend on a fundamental intuition of the following kind. The utilitarian gives priority to the notion of benefit. This means that he would find it plausible to explain the attention we give to so-called rights by saying that we respect rights because this is an important way of benefiting those whose rights are respected. The rights theorist puts matters the other way around. His intuition is that we find it plausible to regard persons as being entitled to be benefited in certain ways only because we have a general conception of persons as being entitled by right to respect and consideration as ends in themselves.

This debate has been and continues to be one of the most provocative and fruitful debates in contemporary philosophy of law. Many issues involving judicial function, legislative function, and the assumptions about human nature made by law are issues that are implicated in this debate. At the same time, positivists remind us that this debate is about the optimal use of an institution, one which can be and has been used in many ways throughout human history. They stress the importance of distinguishing the description of the tool from the description of its uses. They suggest that we must understand the tool before we can understand its uses, and they seek to offer persuasive accounts of law's formal features.

Index

233